LET THE FIRE FALL

Let the Fire Fall

Michael Scanlan, T. O. R.
With
James Manney

SERVANT BOOKS
Ann Arbor, Michigan

Cover design by Charles Piccirilli, Graphicus Corp
Cover photo by Larry George

Nothing Contrary to Faith: Rev. Christian Oravec, T.O.R., S.T.D.
Rev. Daniel Sinisi, T.O.R., M.A., S.T.D.

Approved: Very Rev. Dennis Sullivan, T.O.R.
Minister Provincial

Published by Servant Books
P.O. Box 8617
Ann Arbor, Michigan 48107

10 9 8 7 6 5 4 3 2 1 86 87 88 89 90

Printed in the United States of America
ISBN 0-89283-296-7

Contents

ONE

Free from Fear

THE RINGING TELEPHONE JARRED ME out of sleep, and I groped for my bearings as I grabbed the receiver. Where was I? What city was I in? What day was it?

"Good morning, Fr. Scanlan. This is your wake up call. It's 6:30," said the desk clerk cheerily.

The answers came. I'm in a hotel room. In Chicago. It's Saturday morning.

This was the last morning of a conference for college deans at the University of Chicago. I awoke, prayed, shaved and showered slowly, then packed my suitcase so I could make a quick departure that afternoon. I had had enough of *talking* about being a dean. I was anxious to get back to the College of Steubenville and start being a dean.

I had a reservation on a flight from O'Hare to Pittsburgh, but now my plans were changed. The night before, at half time at a basketball game between Steubenville and DePaul, I ran into John Sala, dean of Bethany College in West Virginia.

"Father Mike," he said. "Let's fly home together."

"Fine," I replied. "What plane are you on?"

"No, I mean let's fly in *my* plane," he said. "I'm a pilot, and my plane is over at the county airport. I'll land across the river from Steubenville, and we'll be home for dinner."

Why not? I wanted to get to know John better. He was a retired Air Force colonel who had gone into college admin-

1

istration as a second career. I, too, had been in the Air Force before entering the Franciscan order. And anyway, I always liked adventure. So off we went by taxi to the county airport as soon as the conference was over.

I had second thoughts about my "adventure" when I took a look at the plane. I was used to flying in large commercial aircraft. In the Air Force I had flown in smaller planes. But John's Piper Cub looked little bigger than a large kite. Did I want to fly 600 miles in a plane called a "cub"?

It was a clear but windy December morning. The wind kicked up as we packed our suitcases in the plane and stuffed ourselves into the two seats. John and I almost rubbed shoulders. A gust of wind buffeted the plane as we taxied out for takeoff. The little Volkswagen I sometimes drove in Steubenville seemed larger and more reliable than this flimsy machine. I said a silent prayer as we slowly took off into the wind—*very* slowly, I thought—and the firm frozen ground dropped away.

I gradually relaxed as we circled south of Chicago and headed across Indiana. Conversation with John helped. It was no more strange for me to be in a little plane on a cold December afternoon than it was for me to be dean of the College of Steubenville. I told John how I, a priest ordained only six months, had come to be a dean, an "instant dean," one of my friends laughed when he heard the improbable news.

I was a dean because my superior had ordered me to become one. For three years I had been preparing to go to South America as a Franciscan missionary. But when I got together with my superior, Fr. Kevin, shortly after my ordination, he said that the College of Steubenville needed an academic dean and that I was the man.

But it was no joke. I was dean. When I asked Kevin what a dean did, he said I would go to a summer course at Catholic University in Washington to find out. I went back to my room in a daze. I really didn't know what a dean was. In all my years in college and at law school, I had never gone to the dean's office. I pulled the dictionary off the shelf and looked up "dean." The book told me that I was about to become "the head of a division, faculty, college, or school of a university."

John was amused as I told him this story while the winter scenery passed beneath the wings of our plane. John was a devoted Protestant. Like most Protestants at the time (and most Catholics today), he could not understand the obedience that was demanded of Catholic clergy in the Catholic church of the day. The tremors from Vatican Council II had already begun to shake the church in 1964, although not to the degree to which they were about to. But priests, especially priests in religious orders, were still accustomed to obeying their superiors with alacrity, and their superiors were accustomed to making assignments without much consideration of their subordinates' wishes or even consultation with them. I had been stunned by Fr. Kevin's decision to make me dean, but I did not think he had acted improperly. Rather, I thought he probably knew God's plan for my life better than I did.

I also thought Kevin was right. I thought I might learn to be a pretty good dean. I was only thirty-four years old. I lacked the PhD that was virtually required for deanship at colleges and universities, and I had been going to conferences like the one in Chicago in an almost frantic attempt to master the job. But I *was* able to make decisions. And, as the president of the college frequently remarked to me, I had so far managed not to make any serious mistakes.

John thought I was doing okay too. He was a veteran academic administrator who had transferred from the Air Force to Bethany College. We chatted happily. He told me about his flying days before moving into the educational division of the Air Force.

A sudden thud of turbulence halted conversation and brought a quick prayer to my lips. "Turbulence" is a fancy word for the little disturbance that airline passengers sometimes feel when riding in a large plane. This turbulence was different: a sudden sickening jolt, as if our plane was a child's toy that the child had kicked across the room. We were near home. Steubenville was only about fifty miles ahead. The sun was sinking in the west behind us. Ahead we could see what looked like a dark cloud lying menacingly across the horizon and obscuring the ground.

John barked into the radio. "What's that cloud ahead?" he asked. He listened for a moment before signing off.

"The Zanesville tower says it's smoke in the Ohio Valley and not to worry," he told me. We flew on toward the cloud.

The turbulence increased as we approached it. John gripped the controls apprehensively as we flew on. He suspected now that the cloud was something far worse than air pollution, but it was too late to turn back. The plane's nose touched the darkness.

It was a ferocious hailstorm. A cascade of hailstones, all sounding as large and solid as golf balls, rattled against the thin skin of the Piper Cub, inches from my head. The wind roared. I once saw a cat toying with a small trapped mouse. It swatted the mouse carelessly to and fro, knocking the little creature back whenever it tried to escape. The wind played with us like the cat with the mouse. We lurched up a few score feet, then we dropped a few hundred in seconds. The gale shook us to the left, then to the right. The ground disappeared once we got in the cloud, and the plane's night lights came on. I saw to my horror that the fragile wings of the plane were flapping up and down wildly. John yelled and groaned.

The cat killed the mouse after playing with it. I knew we were about to die.

My life was over. All that was left was the actual dying. Emotion raced through me—but only for a moment. With death assured there was nothing to be afraid of. I didn't really experience fear. Fear has something to do with uncertainty; you're afraid that something bad *might* happen to you, that you *might* die. I *knew* that death was staring me right in the face. There was nothing to be afraid of. My life on earth was over.

I turned to the Lord. "Lord Jesus, I've done many things I wish I hadn't done. I haven't done many things I wish I had. I'm sorry." As the hail battered and the wind roared and the plane spun down toward the ground I couldn't see but knew was there, I said, "Lord, I give it all to you, and I trust in your merciful love."

At that instant I experienced an extraordinary visitation of God. I was enveloped in God's love. It filled every fiber of my heart. Peace welled up within me. The mind can play tricks in desperate situations, but this was no trick. The Lord God almighty was *there*—there in that ridiculously small plane which was about to crash in a field somewhere west of Steubenville, Ohio. I was completely indifferent to death. All I cared about was the Lord and going to meet him in a matter of seconds. That was more real to me than the rattle of the hail that I heard in my ears as the plane fell.

John looked at me at a time when our lives could be measured in seconds. I was grinning, he told me later. "I was sure you had flipped out." He made one last desperate maneuver. He put the plane into a dive. He told me later that he recalled reading somewhere in his Air Force training that a gust of wind at the bottom of a hailstorm can take you out and across to safety.

The book was right. The gale pulled us out of the dive about 500 feet above the ground, and we slid east far enough to get our bearings and make an emergency landing in Zanesville. Hail had turned to snow at the Zanesville airport. I watched the snowflakes hit my shoe as I walked from the plane to the tiny terminal. The air was cold and my heart was still racing. I was amazed to be alive. I was glad but a little disappointed, too. Then I felt funny about being disappointed.

The truth was that I was indifferent to death. I knew what Paul meant when he wrote, to live or die is naught because I have the Lord Jesus.

Later I read a poem by Blaise Pascal that captured the essence of the experience of peace I had in that little Piper Cub as it spun down to the hard earth. The poem, called "Fire," recounted his own experience. The poet prays:

> God of Abraham, God of Isaac, God of Jacob,
>   not of the philosophers and scholars.
> Certitude. Certitude. Feeling. Joy. Peace.
> God of Jesus Christ.
> "Thy God shall be my God."
> Forgetfulness of the world and of everything,
>   except God.

"Forgetfulness of everything except God." I have done many things and had many experiences in the twenty years since I nearly died in the hailstorm. The Lord saw fit to spare me that time. I now understand that my death was merely postponed. Soon my earthly life will end; yours will, too. Then I will go and be with the Lord. Life with Christ. That's the important thing. Soon it will be the only thing.

My brush with death in the skies caused me to think differently about why we are here on earth. We are destined to spend eternity with the Lord. He has saved us and connected us to his church. He has given us work to do. He wants our marriages and families and jobs to work well. But why, exactly? What are we here for? What is the importance of the brief time we spend on this earth, doing the particular work we do within the particular set of relationships we have?

I have come to see, more clearly than anything else, the imminent drama of life. A savage war is raging, and we are part of it. The work we do is of eternal importance because, like it or not, people will have eternal happiness or eternal misery according to what *we* do. Every person we work with, talk to, and pass on the street is a spiritual being who will live forever. Spiritual armies are arrayed in the heavens, on the earth, and in our hearts to seize territory. We are both the soldiers in the battle and the battleground the war is fought on.

What will we talk about in heaven? We will talk about the war and the role we played in it.

I do not go about my daily tasks with the grim intensity of a soldier under hostile fire. I have also come to see that we can have perfect joy in the midst of troubles, and that the battle can be fought with grace and peace. This is something that St. Francis, the founder of my order, demonstrated to the world more clearly than any other follower of the Lord. All that mattered to Francis was being in Jesus Christ. That's all that should matter to us.

Jesus Christ frees us. I have seen him free thousands of men and women from diseases, afflictions, addictions, and the consequences of emotional distress. He has freed me. As that little plane spun toward the ground over Ohio and I was sure my life expectancy could be measured in minutes, he freed me from a great burden of fear that had blighted my life. I recall reading the climactic lines in Stephen Crane's *The Red Badge of Courage,* where the hero reflects that The Great Death is after all only the great death. As I overcame my fear of death, the Lord lifted fear from me.

Fear had always been with me—fear that I could not measure up, fear that I would be inadequate to do the job at hand, fear that I would fail, fear that I would be rejected. I left my fear somewhere in the skies over Ohio. When the Lord visited me and showed me how to face death itself calmly, even joyfully, fear vanished. It seemed that once I could welcome death, there was nothing left to fear. Oh, I feel apprehension sometimes—as I go to a hospital to minister to a dying boy and his family, as I get ready to address thousands of people at a rally, when I look at deficit budget projections for programs at the University of Steubenville. But I do not feel fear. In fact, the apprehension rarely lasts very long.

The truth is that God is with us. A better way to say it is that we are with God. He wants to do more for us than we can imagine. I have written this book to illustrate these few simple truths.

This book is about what God can do for you. I am going to tell stories about my life and stories about people I've known or heard about. They are invitations to turn to the Lord more radically, to drink of his Holy Spirit more deeply, and to allow yourself to be used by him more powerfully than you ever have before.

I write with a sense of urgency. There's a war going on, people are dying, and many of us are asleep.

TWO

In the Woods

W HO IS GOD? What could I know about him? What was my
relationship with him?

I learned the catechism answers to these questions very well
while growing up in Catholic boarding schools. But the
answers and the doctrines weren't enough. I had my first hint
of a personal encounter with God in a place where few
eighteen-year-olds were found—on board a freighter that
carried machine tools, buses, textiles, and food back and forth
between the United States and a Europe still recovering from
the devastation of World War II.

The year was 1950. I had finished my first year at college and
I wanted a different kind of summer job. I was eager to live up
to an image I had of myself as someone who went everywhere
and did everything. My uncle pulled some strings, and in May,
1950, I shipped out of New York Harbor on the U.S.S.
Steelmaker, a freighter that had carried troops to Europe
during the war and had then returned to its humble job of
carrying cargo across the oceans.

As an ordinary seaman, I was assigned to the least desirable
watch—midnight to 4 A.M. For me, it was the best watch I
could have had. Every night I would awaken from a nap about
11 P.M. and get ready for my night watch, which usually
consisted of sitting in the bow of the ship and looking at the
sea and stars.

The glory of it!

I gazed at the thousands of stars in endless space, so far away that my mind could not grasp the distances, yet so close I thought I could reach out and touch them. I was alone on this vast ocean. Yet this ocean was a small part of a small planet that was but a speck in the cosmos. By temperament I am not exactly a placid and humble person. In school and in life generally I had been a hard worker who thought he had to make things happen, the quicker the better. But here at sea, gazing at the stars and contemplating the astonishing beauty of the night, I felt insignificant. I understood the psalmist: "When I behold your heavens, the work of your fingers, the moon and stars which you set in place, what is man that you should be mindful of him?"

This acknowledgment of my insignificance was the beginning of wisdom. In the grandeur of those summer nights on the ocean I began to sense the presence of God. The psalmist who asked how God could give a thought to man also said, "Praise him, sun and moon, praise him, all you shining stars." For me, an adolescent during the summer after his freshman year of college, the stars were giving powerful testimony to God.

This natural magnificence subdued my restless mind for a time, but eventually it awoke and began probing. I wanted to know the meaning of it all. What was the purpose of my life? Was this world going anywhere? Did it matter what I did? I was convinced that God was behind the creation I was experiencing, but I did not know what that meant or who he was. I had the glimmer of an answer, not the Answer itself.

I was raised to be an achiever in a rather difficult home environment. I was born in Cedarhurst, Long Island, in 1931, and lived for six years in Scanlan Gardens, an apartment house that my father owned and liked so well that he put his name on it. However, my parents separated when I was three years old. My father settled in Mexico and worked in the import-export business. My mother stayed in the New York City area. When I was fourteen, she married Bill Robertson, a hard-working executive for a New York garment manufacturer.

My family was neither wealthy nor socially prominent, and I had the mixed feelings about both money and social position that were typical of many "lace curtain" Irish families of my generation. On the one hand, I was taught to distrust the rich. My friends in school were tough Irish kids. We had nothing but disdain for those who flaunted their money and thought they were better than we were. On the other hand, success was very important to my parents and Bill. There was never much money around, but they liked to live as if there was.

The apartment that Bill and my mother lived in symbolized the ambivalence about success that characterized my childhood. The apartment was at 50 Park Avenue in New York City, a socially impressive, upscale address. However, Bill's employer paid the rent, and I slept on a rollout bed in the living room when I came home from boarding school.

Being a Catholic was an important part of my identity, but I did not have the same Catholic upbringing that other New York Irish-American kids received. There had been no annulment of my parents' marriage, so my mother's second marriage was not recognized in the eyes of the Catholic church. She formed a strong Catholic identity in me and always insisted that I go to Mass and fulfill my other religious obligations faithfully. But she was sporadic in her church attendance when I wasn't home. Instead she would say private prayers. Bill was hostile to the Catholic church, partly, I suspect, because my mother's separation from the church grieved her so much. He would ridicule Catholic doctrine and try to turn me away from the church. I would argue back while my mother suffered the agony of it. I learned to defend my faith at an early age. It was training that served me well in later years.

The man who influenced my religious formation more than anyone else was Brother Bertin Ryan, S.C., a teaching brother who taught me at Coindre Hall, a boarding school that the Brothers of the Sacred Heart operated in Huntington, Long Island. I attended Coindre Hall for five years. Brother Bertin combined the highest standards for personal conduct and academic performance with an irresistible loving nature. He was the first man who ever hugged me, and he hugged me often. At the same time, he would correct me for the slightest infraction of the rules. He was especially perturbed when I failed to do my best.

The memory of one incident involving Brother Bertin has stayed with me all my life. At Coindre Hall we were seated in class according to our academic rank. I was in the first seat for a long time. But at one point I started to fool around and I fell back to the fourth or fifth seat. Brother Bertin took me aside and told me that he was terribly disappointed in me. He wasn't angry so much as deeply hurt. That broke me. I immediately changed my ways, buckled down in my studies, and was soon back in the first seat.

Brother Bertin gave me a thirst for reading and instilled in me a love for sacred things. He gave me a good Catholic education. It turned out to be the last formal Catholic education I would have until I entered the seminary more than twelve years after leaving Coindre Hall.

My parents and teachers raised me to be an achiever. They took it for granted that I would be the best. My mother in particular drummed it into me that I could accomplish anything I wanted to do, achieve anything I was willing to sacrifice for. There was never any limit to what I could accomplish. If I got a 95 on a test, I was asked why I didn't get 100. I was always told it was a matter of willpower. If I tried hard enough, I could do anything.

My restlessness saved me from the crash that certainly awaited me if I had pursued perfectionism. Occasionally I would get discouraged when I failed, but mostly I kept changing what I wanted to do. I decided that I could do anything, but not everything. I could live with lower grades if my goal for a semester was to become captain of the tennis team, as I did in prep school, or to become socially popular, as I strived to do in college. If a course bored me, I would settle for a *B*.

Nevertheless, I was usually on top. I graduated in the top three of my class in grammar school and won a scholarship to prep school. I did very well in New Hampton Prep in New Hampshire and graduated with both the top academic average and the all-around excellence medal.

I decided to go to Williams College in Massachusetts for two reasons: It promised to give me a great intellectual challenge, and it was a place where I could play many sports. My parents were happy with Williams because it was a prestigious small college in the Ivy League tradition. My mother had her heart set on my becoming a great public figure. She would embarrass me by telling me that I should be president of the United States. She was delighted when she later discovered that Harvard Law School accepted propor-tionately more applicants from Williams than from any other college in the United States.

I was also trained to be a fighter as well as an achiever.

In my high school and early college years, I liked to think of myself as someone who could take care of himself, or, better, would never let himself be bullied. I had tough Irish uncles, and I liked to talk tough around my buddies in grammar school, but the only real street fight I ever got into was a fiasco.

It happened in New York City one fall evening. I was leaving a dance when my friends and I encountered a group of drunken football players on a Manhattan street. They were from a college in the Midwest, and they were either cele-brating or drowning their sorrows in alcohol after a game in the area. They made a comic sight, dressed in their school colors, singing college fight songs late at night. As I passed one huge celebrant, I chuckled. He called me a name. I laughed again.

I woke up in the gutter. The next few minutes are hazy, too. People who were with me said that the football player knocked me out with one punch. Apparently, I got up and ran around looking for him. I was lucky that he had run away.

I was more successful as a fighter for my faith. After

grammar school, very little in my life supported a Catholic identity. Most of the students and faculty at New Hampton Prep and Williams College were secularized people with Christian backgrounds. Many were downright antagonistic to Christian beliefs. Bill Robertson and I would argue about religion when I came home for visits. I learned that if I was to be a Catholic, I would have to defend myself.

I learned this lesson in the most literal way possible during my summer job on the U.S.S. *Steelmaker*. The veteran seamen I shipped out with were amused by my Catholic beliefs, and they took it as a personal challenge to lead me into sin when we arrived in port. I stoutly resisted temptation and told them why. For this or some other reason unknown to me the seaman sleeping in the bunk beneath mine would grab me every night by the throat and say, "Junior, I'm going to kill you." Then he would climb into his bunk; and I would fall asleep wondering if he would ever carry out his threat.

But this opposition made me strong in my faith. I learned early a very important lesson—that it costs something to follow the Lord. As individuals, we must painfully surrender ourselves to the Lord. But this is also true socially. If we take our beliefs seriously, people will mock us and oppose us.

At the same time, I did not really believe the gospel with a burning personal conviction. I thought of myself as a good Catholic, but as I went through college I was still grappling with those questions that I wrestled with on the bow of the ship. How could man be so infinitesimal, yet loved by God? How could God be so majestic and awesome, and yet accessible to us? I suspected the answers lay in the long tradition of Christian doctrine and worship, but I could not fit it together. I believed, yet I was not sure about the Person I said I believed in. It was more like I believed that I ought to believe.

The problem was that my faith was not my own. It was the faith of other people. This faith had been handed down to me, but I had yet to assimilate it, to take it into myself, to make it Mike Scanlan's faith.

A borrowed faith like mine is inevitably tested. Appropriately enough, for a young man who took the stance of a defender of the faith, my testing came through a philosophy class.

The class, which was strongly recommended for every student at Williams, was taught by a brilliant ex-Catholic named Miller. Williams College stressed systematic doubt as a way of approaching all studies. Almost every professor taught us to doubt every proposition that anyone advanced. This skepticism reached its fullest development in Professor Miller's third-year philosophy class. Where other professors taught us to doubt the pronouncements of experts and critics, Miller taught us to doubt even our own existence.

Miller began with the basic stuff of thinking. He rejected the purely spiritualist and naturalist approaches to existence. Then he moved on to the epistomology: How do you know what you know? He taught us to ask questions like, "How do you know you won't wake up and discover that what you think is real is no more real than your last good dream?"

By late fall, 1950, this class had moved me to such a profound level of doubt and relativity that I wasn't sure of anything. Is everything an illusion? Was I real? Was anything else real? Even if I instinctively believed in the reality of the material world, how could I prove it? I didn't think I could. My beliefs seemed like simple prejudices, arbitrary ideas that I chose to hang on to because I wasn't courageous enough to do without them.

This included my belief in God. Miller dismissed such beliefs as meaningless. I wondered if he was right. If I couldn't prove that *I* exist, what chance did I have of proving that God existed? That sense of awe and power I had felt in the bow of the boat at night that summer after my freshman year seemed just that—senses and feelings disconnected from reason. Intellectually, I was wallowing.

I had the good sense to realize that the answer had to come from God, not from my confused mind. On the night before my twentieth birthday, December 1, 1950, I decided to take the next day off and go to God. I bundled up in warm clothing the next morning, took a notebook and pen, and went off into the woods near the campus. I told God my predicament as well as I could. I was too much the confused student to really cry out to God. I knew that he understood my problem better than I did—that is, if he existed. So I simply said something like this: "I know you don't want me to be so confused, so lost, so uncertain about everything. Especially about you. If you are there, will you let me know?"

To let God know how serious I was, I vowed to stay in the woods until he made things clear.

It sounds like I was challenging God, almost putting him to the test. My "prayer" does, in fact, have an element of youthful bravado in it. But it was the right prayer to pray. I know that God led me to do it. If you are confused or doubting, seek the Lord. He who seeks will find. The door will be opened to him who knocks. The sincere prayer of the seeker will be answered.

My prayer was not answered for half a day. I stomped around the woods all morning and into the afternoon, listening, writing, and trying to keep warm. I heard nothing from God. The winter sun set in late afternoon. It got dark and cold. I was hungry. Curiously, I was not too uncomfortable. I was not inclined to give up and conclude that the radical skeptics and anti-supernatural materialists in my philosophy class were right after all.

Then, about 9:30 at night, in the cold and darkness of the woods, I suddenly became a believer. My spirit was moved by God himself; he visited me. I was very quickly and very unexpectedly filled with faith. I believed in Jesus Christ, the Son of God. I believed that he founded a church, one that I could trust and give my whole life to. I grasped the *truth*. The truth was a block of revelation that I could base my whole life on. I left the woods a believer, never to doubt the truth of the Christian faith again.

My infilling with faith was important for what it *wasn't*. It wasn't something that I had conjured up on my own. I had spent a good part of the preceding twelve hours trying to make something happen in my relationship with God. I did this in the best way I knew how—by using my mind, by reasoning, and by asking subtle questions.

Neither was the experience something I achieved through heroic prayer. I talked about prayer far more than I prayed in those days. There was nothing particularly prayerful about my day in the woods. It was hard to pray to an abstract God whose existence I doubted.

No, my experience in the woods was something *God* did. Only after I stopped thinking and straining to understand did he act. That was the point of it. He takes the initiative with us. We need God. He reaches out to us in our need when we turn to him in simplicity. When we reach the end of our resources, he acts.

Many years later, I read the accounts of a man named Francis Gajowniczek, a Pole who was visiting a Polish town in western Pennsylvania. Less than ten years before my walk in the woods, Francis Gajowniczek was a condemned man on his way to death at the Auschwitz concentration camp. A prisoner had escaped; the Nazis had decided that ten Polish prisoners would be starved to death in retribution. The ten men were chosen at random. Francis was among them, a dead man, without hope.

As the men were being led off to the starvation cells, Francis cried out, "What will happen to my wife and children?" A little priest named Maximilian Kolbe ran up and begged the commandant to let him take Francis's place. Why? the Nazi asked. "I am a priest," replied Kolbe. Scornfully, the commandant ordered the substitution made. Fr. Kolbe died in Francis's place.

Maximilian Kolbe is now a saint of the church. Francis Gajowniczek honors the man who died to save him. Everywhere he goes, Francis shows the concentration camp number 5659 tattooed on his arm. It reminds him, he says, of his condemnation, of the time when he had no hope but was saved.

Francis Gajowniczek stands for all of us. Like him, we were condemned. We had no hope. We were being marched away to death when another, moved by love and compassion, offered himself as a sacrifice in our place. Like Francis, we did absolutely nothing to deserve or earn our rescue. Like Francis, we are all called to love, serve, honor, and obey the One who saved us.

This is what I came to understand in the woods. My situation became clear to me. I was heading for oblivion. I was a sinner, lost, without hope. My good mind, my well-exercised body, my fine intentions, my noble dreams—nothing of my own could do anything to change these facts. Yet I also saw clearly that God had done something awesome and unexpected about my condition. He had taken on human flesh and offered himself as the ransom for my sins. Furthermore, he had established a church which was his body and which continued his work of salvation on earth.

All this I saw with eyes of faith. People often talk about faith as if it were some exotic mystery or a capacity acquired after years of searching. For me, faith is simply a way of seeing. In fact, the experience of receiving faith that evening in the woods was a lot like putting on a pair of glasses and being able to see clearly for the first time. If you are nearsighted, you know what I mean. Without your glasses you can see, but not well. You have some idea of what's out there, but you are not sure.

If you were nearsighted and had never worn glasses, you would not know that you could not really see. You had been bothered by the nagging feeling that something was not right. Then when you put your glasses on, everything suddenly became clear. It was like a whole new world opening up to you, a world with sharp edges and vivid colors and intriguing details.

That's what receiving faith was like for me. I had had a basic Catholic education, but I didn't see the truth clearly. I glimpsed the truth, but the truth wasn't alive in me. I had even begun to doubt that the truth was real. With faith, I could *see*. Skepticism and doubt were the illusion. The truth was the gospel of Jesus Christ, the rock I could build my life on.

Faith also enabled me to look back and fully appreciate my Catholic education. The writer of Hebrews defines faith as "confident assurance concerning what we hope for, and conviction about things we do not see." He then goes on to reassure his readers, a community of Jewish Christians undergoing persecution, that their faith would be rewarded. He does this by showing how faith bore great fruit in the lives of their forefathers—Noah and Abraham, Isaac and Moses, David and Samuel and all the rest.

Something similar happened to me in the months and years after receiving faith in the woods near Williams College. I had a great hunger to *learn* about my faith. I read everything about Catholicism and Christianity that anyone recommended. I pored over catechisms. I read the Catholic press. I read all the booklets in the racks in back of church. I began to sense the great richness of the spiritual treasures that had been handed down through the centuries.

I *had* to learn about my faith because my newly strengthened beliefs were immediately challenged. I was known in my fraternity for defending Catholic teaching. Sometimes this notoriety was comic. One evening two fraternity brothers got into an argument over whether I could go to bed with my fiancée and still adhere to orthodox Catholic teaching. One said yes; the other said no. No one asked me what I thought— of course I knew I couldn't do such a thing—but the debate went on for a considerable time.

But I also had to seriously defend my faith. My debate coach, an ex-Catholic, liked to assign me to defend unpopular Catholic issues like the immorality of artificial birth control and whether the United States should send an ambassador to the Vatican.

I also got myself elected president of the Newman Club on campus, the beginnings of my involvement in leadership of Catholic institutions. I identified strongly with Catholic writers like Chesterton and Newman, who had been adult converts. They had been tested, I thought, just as I was being tested.

I graduated from Williams and headed for Harvard Law School, the gateway to power and success, the place where the best competed with each other. I wanted to be tested, and I thought Harvard was the most challenging academic test I could encounter.

I wondered what God wanted of me in the future. After describing Abraham, Jacob, Moses, and the other great giants of faith, the writer of Hebrews makes a statement that must have been reassuring to his readers and that sounds startling to us. "God had made a better plan," the writer concludes, "a plan which includes us."

What plan did God have for me?

THREE

Vocation

WHEN YOU FIND OUT HOW FAR YOU CAN GO, you've gone too far. In my second year of law school, I went too far. I tried to become the top student at Harvard Law School. I ended up in the infirmary with flu and exhaustion. I didn't make the top, but I was satisfied with making one final attempt to do something I had come to Harvard to do.

I came to Harvard looking for the biggest challenge I could find. My academic record at Williams was good but not spectacular. That bothered me. I wanted to be stretched. I didn't want someone to say in twenty or thirty years, "You know, Scanlan, you had great potential but you never fulfilled it." I came to Harvard primarily because it was the place where the best people competed with each other.

So in my second year, I went for it. I studied all the time. I stayed in Cambridge during vacations and devoted myself to studies. Except for an hour of exercise most days, a party on Saturday night, and Mass on Sunday, I would eat, drink, breathe, and dream about the law.

The results were conclusive. I couldn't sustain the experiment long enough. I was hospitalized with flu and exhaustion. I did well academically. I even got a few *A*'s, which were almost impossible to get. But I wasn't the best, and no amount of discipline and study could make me the best. After finding out how far I could go, I relaxed. I enjoyed the last year of law school more than the first two.

When I arrived at Harvard I was not terribly interested in discovering God's plan for my life. I was much more concerned with *my* plan.

My plan was to be the best I could be. My career goals were a little vague, but I wanted to go in a certain direction—toward politics and government. I did not want to run for office but rather to advise and influence those who did. What was my dream? When I let my imagination go, I saw myself as the chief of staff for the president of the United States, the right-hand man for the most powerful man in the world.

This dream was not entirely fantasy. President Theodore Roosevelt had gone to Harvard. So had a young and politically ambitious senator from Massachusetts named John F. Kennedy, who, it was rumored, had his eye on higher office. For some people, Harvard Law School provided a superior legal education. For others, it was the gateway to wealth. For many of us, including me, it was the entree to power and influence. Some of my classmates could well be future cabinet officers, ambassadors, presidential assistants, possibly even one was a future president. I was here to make my mark among these people.

From my first day at Harvard, I devoted myself to my work as single-mindedly as a contemplative monk devotes himself to prayer and knowledge of God. On a rare weekend I would see the woman I was privately engaged to, but she was in Saratoga Springs, New York, and I was into law. I was obsessed with being the best. I thought that God fully endorsed my way of life. Why wouldn't he approve? I thought. I was only trying to use the gifts he had given me to their fullest.

Or so I told myself. In my more honest moments, I conceded that my constant studying flowed from mixed and tainted motives. I *said* I wanted to do well with God's gifts. But I also wanted to please *me*. I wanted to be better than others, and I wanted other people to recognize that I was better than they were. If necessary, others would have to fail so that I could be best.

I was disgusted with myself when I saw that I was driven by such motives and unruly desires. One morning in late winter of my first year, I woke up, went into the bathroom, and looked at myself in the mirror. It sounds like a cliche, but I just hated what I saw: an opportunistic young law student, wholly given over to a process and a system that was turning him into a very unpleasant character.

My fiancée had just recently confronted me with the painful truth. She told me that she hated what I was becoming. I knew she was right, but only now was I willing to face it.

Where was God in this frantic rat race of a life, this never-ending round of note-taking, cramming and anxious competition, of irresponsible partying and constant self-concern? I didn't doubt that the Lord wanted me to go to law school. I wanted to know what he wanted me to do with my law degree. Most of all, I wanted *him*.

I recalled the closeness to the Lord that I had felt that evening in the woods and throughout my last years at Williams College. It was a distant memory. I also recalled that conviction I had had at Williams that I was doing what he wanted. That was a memory, too. At Williams I had been an outspoken Catholic and had taken great pleasure in being one, because I felt utterly secure in my identity as a son of God, a man saved by Jesus Christ, destined to spend eternity with him. Now I wasn't so sure who I was or where I was going. I was only sure that the Lord wasn't happy about it.

I decided to take Lent seriously. The traditional Catholic observance of Lent was fairly rigorous in those days. The rules required us to fast between meals and to eat two small meals a day. I decided to do that. I would also go to daily Mass and say a daily rosary. I would take this season of repentance and self-examination as a time to evaluate my life and to hear God's word to me.

Lent began and I started my round of fasting, prayer, and Mass. I immediately noticed one effect: My Lenten disciplines got my attention off exclusive concern with my studies. I still went to lectures, took notes, and put in my time in the library, but the anxiety was gone. The law no longer absorbed my life. My heart was still restless, but it was restless for something far more important than success in the law.

One morning toward the end of the second week of Lent, I was walking back to the law school after early Mass at the Catholic church in North Cambridge. I wasn't especially aware of my surroundings; surely I was not expecting anything to happen. I think I was musing about the class I was attending next. I decided to take a short cut that I often took across the grounds of the home of Henry Wadsworth Longfellow, the nineteenth-century poet. Longfellow's big white Victorian house was a local landmark and museum. A path across his property was a shortcut from the Catholic church to the apartment I shared with three other students. Without thinking about it, I started down the deserted path.

After a few steps, I stopped—paralyzed. I could not have moved if I had wanted to. But I did not want to, for I was experiencing an overwhelming sense of God's presence and power. I understood why the prophets use such fantastic imagery when they describe encounters with God. Isaiah saw the Lord coming on a throne surrounded by seraphim with six wings. Ezekiel saw the Lord in a vision of a mighty, gleaming, flashing cloud full of fire and jewels and strange marvels. All this is a poor attempt to put in words the indescribable awe and strangeness of an encounter with the living God. He was *there*—before me, in me, over me.

Then the Lord "spoke." He did not speak precisely in audible sounds but with a distinct voice that was more real to me than the human voices I had heard all my life. It was a "voice" inside me. It said, simply, "Will you give me your whole life?"

Now my mind was as paralyzed as my body. I didn't want to

say yes or no. I thought, clumsily, that I certainly didn't want to say no, would not say no, to an invitation from God no matter how frightening it seemed to be. But it was a terribly frightening question. I didn't want to say yes either. My whole life? My *whole* life? Literally my *life*? When confronted by God in similar situations many generations ago, Jeremiah objected that he was inarticulate and too young, and Isaiah merely wept, "Woe is me, I am doomed." I understood.

"What do you mean, Lord?" I asked.

"Will you give me your whole life?" he asked again.

I had a strong sense that the Lord was offering me a real choice that didn't involve my salvation. I could say no and go on and lead a fruitful and productive life as a good Catholic that would nevertheless not be the kind of life I could have had if I had surrendered to the Lord completely. Did I want that? Not only did I dislike the idea of saying no to God for any reason, but I rebelled at the prospect of settling for anything less than the top and the best. The Lord could deal with my pride and my ambition later. For now, this aspect of my personality served me well, for I was too proud to say anything but yes.

Nevertheless, I bargained with God. Abraham negotiated to save Sodom. Moses tried to cut a deal to get out of the job of leading the Hebrew people out of Egypt. Scanlan bargained with God to save his mother's and father's feelings.

"I will give you my whole life, Lord," I said. "But I would like to finish law school." My mother and father had their hearts set on my becoming a successful lawyer. My father had put up thousands of dollars to send me to Harvard. *No one* would understand if I dropped out of Harvard now. All this ran quickly through my mind as I stood paralyzed on the path. "As soon as I am qualified as a lawyer, then I will do what you want," I said.

I am surprised and a little ashamed at my audacity. Jesus told an ominous parable about people like me—the parable of the master who grew angry when his dinner guests turned down his invitation. They had good excuses, but he rejected them all. Not even being newly married was a sufficient excuse for not coming. "Not one of those invited shall taste a morsel of my dinner," the master said, and he sent his servant out into the highways and byways to invite the poor, the crippled, and the blind.

I did not think of the parable. Indeed, I thought the Lord accepted the condition. I sensed that he, too, wanted me to become a lawyer.

The presence of God left me, and I resumed my walk across Longfellow's lawn and on to class. I was shaken. I had the impression that my conversation with God about my future was merely interrupted for a while. He still had to tell me what he wanted me to do.

I suspected that he wanted me to be a priest. This was 1954. Catholics in those days grew up with the idea that men who were *really* serious about serving God became priests. Since God had visited me so personally, I thought I was destined to be a missionary priest—the most dedicated life of service I could think of. How did becoming a lawyer fit into *that*? I wondered.

Many questions remained to be answered. But I had no doubt that they *would* be answered, and that thought filled me with peace and joy. I was still bothered about many things, but the turmoil in my life over my future was over.

A few months after the encounter with God on Longfellow's property I reflected on God's goodness. How good God was to me! I had made a very simple and not very demanding decision to be faithful to a few Lenten disciplines. I simply sought him. I had not gone on a heroic fast or rearranged my life in a dramatic way in order to make something happen. *He* had made things happen. He had revealed himself to me, given me a call, actually spoken to me in a way that I could not mistake.

Years later I got to know Charles Colson, an ambitious man who had experienced a profound conversion after living at the pinnacle of power in the White House. Colson has a sign on his desk that says, "Faithfulness Not Success." That's it exactly. Our call is to be faithful, not successful. The secret is simple obedience. God will do the rest.

Obedience may be simple, but it's not always easy. In the aftermath of my encounter with God in Cambridge I realized that I had to break my engagement. This task was made doubly difficult by the fact that I did not think I could tell Joy why we had to part. I did not know how to speak about my encounter with God in a way that she or anyone else could understand. In fact, it was years before I told anyone about what happened that afternoon on Longfellow's property. It was too personal and too tentative. The conversation had been interrupted, not completed. I simply didn't know what the future held.

So I had the painful conversation with Joy at the end of the semester. It was one of the hardest things I ever did. She raised the issue by saying we should marry now or end the relationship. I settled it by telling her we should part ways. We parted amicably but painfully. After I last spoke to her I cried for two hours. Later I wrote her to thank her for releasing in me the capacity to love.

That summer I worked as a night elevator operator in New York. The job left me with plenty of time on my hands and I used it to read many of the spiritual classics: Newman and Chesterton, a bit of Augustine and a little Aquinas, and then a lot of Tolstoy.

I was recovering from my meeting with the Lord and its aftermath. I was also getting ready for what lay ahead.

And I was learning that following the Lord can exact a heavy price.

FOUR

Priest

I BM USED TO HAVE A TELEVISION COMMERCIAL that told small businessmen that its personal computer business software would help them "get your ducks in a row." It shows a comic Charlie Chaplin figure ushering a row of ducks out a door in a perfectly straight line.

By the end of Harvard Law School I had all my ducks in a row for a prosperous, successful career as a lawyer. I had the right schools, the right education, the right experience, the right friends. But even though the direction of my life looked clear from the world's point of view, it wasn't clear at all. I felt like the comic figure in the TV commercial leading the ducks but not really knowing the way. I had given my life over completely to God. He had yet to tell me what that meant. I strongly suspected it meant my life wouldn't turn out the way everyone else suspected it would.

Meanwhile, I enjoyed all the attention that recruiters paid to someone who finished in the top quarter of the graduating class at Harvard Law School. New York law firms came calling with tempting, lucrative job offers. I tentatively accepted an offer from the prestigious firm of Patterson, Belknap, and Webb, located at 1 Wall Street. The partner who recruited me promised me an opportunity to reach the top of the legal profession in a firm that worked on the legal problems of some of the nation's largest corporations and wealthiest executives.

Politics beckoned too. Senator John Kennedy of Massachusetts was putting together a team for the national campaign he was to eventually make in 1960. The national headquarters was to be in New York, the nation's financial and media capital, and I was asked to join a group of Ivy League lawyers who would work there on Kennedy's presidential plans. It was the kind of inside political job that could lead to great power if the candidate was successful.

First, however, I would have to do my military service. I had joined the Air Force ROTC in college, thinking I would rather be a college graduate serving as an officer in the Air Force than a private drafted out of college into the army. My two years active service obligation had been delayed for law school, and the Air Force would be quite happy to put a newly graduated lawyer to work. I would go into the Judge Advocate Corps, the Air Force's legal arm. I would be based in Washington, D.C., and would prosecute and defend Air Force personnel accused of crimes in the Air Defense Command from Delaware to North Carolina. It would be excellent legal experience of the kind I could not get in civilian life.

Yet I was somewhat detached from all this. I was waiting for God's plan for me to unfold. A few years previously I would have been thrilled at choosing between a prestigious Wall Street law firm and a possible future president's political team. But now I knew that God would eventually tell me what it meant that I had given my whole life to him.

I was amazed that God himself would speak to me. Think about it. The God who created the universe, who set the stars in their place, who is mightier than the fiercest storm on the greatest ocean, the God who rules the limitless cosmos—this God speaks to *you*. He is interested in you personally. He wants your life to work well. He has a *plan* for your life and he wants to tell you about it.

Isn't that amazing?

But it's true. God created men and women to have close

fellowship with him. When Adam and Eve walked with God in the garden, they spoke intimately and frequently, as a father and his children do. Their sin shattered man's ability to speak to God and hear his voice. Man's situation was tragic: he was created to speak with and hear God in a close personal way, but he was no longer able to do so.

God slowly restored us to this position of closeness to him. He started with particular people. He told Noah to build an ark, and Noah heard him and obeyed. He told Abraham to leave his land and found a new nation, and Abraham obeyed. God spoke to Moses many times about his plan for his chosen people, and Moses heard him and relayed his words to the Israelites.

God had so much to say to the people through Moses that Moses could not do the job alone. One day Jethro, his father-in-law, observed Moses ministering to a large crowd of people who had a need to hear God's word for them, just as we all do. Jethro stated the obvious: This system wasn't working. Moses was wearing himself out giving God's word to each individual Jew. Other needs were not being tended to. Jethro suggested that Moses appoint elders to pastor the people. Moses asked the Lord about this idea.

The Lord said that was his plan, too, and furthermore, he would give a portion of his Spirit to each of the elders. The Spirit fell. It even fell on two elders who were not present for the anointing by Moses. When asked about this, Moses said a wonderful thing: "Would that all of my people were prophets."

Our deepest desire—the desire to know God and to hear his voice—was fulfilled at Pentecost. God poured out his Spirit on all flesh and once again made it possible for us to walk and talk with him. He did what he promised Jeremiah he would do: "I will place my law within them and write it upon their hearts."

It's a remarkable fact: Those of us who are in the Lord can hear his word for our lives.

During my law school years, I had come to understand how

important it was that I discern the Lord's plan for my life. But discerning his plan was not easy. I wrestled with the same questions about guidance that we all struggle with. How do we grow in hearing God's word? How do we distinguish between God's word and our own thoughts, even our "inspired" thoughts?

The answer is that as we get to know the Lord better, we are better able to discern what is from him and what isn't. Hearing the Lord depends on the closeness of our relationship with him.

How do we grow in a relationship with the Lord? We study Scripture. The God who speaks to you is the same God who speaks in the pages of the Bible. We study the fathers of the church and the lives of the saints. We hear God in how he manifests himself in those who have preceded us. We follow the teachings of the church, guarding our hearts and minds. We celebrate Mass and make frequent use of the Eucharist and the other sacraments. These are means which he intends us to use to know him more deeply and love him more.

Most of all, we pray. The Lord wants us to take a time each day to worship him, to thank him, and to listen for his voice. When we don't have answers for our lives, we keep asking the Lord our questions, confident that he will not fail us.

As you do these things, you will come to hear God's word for you. You will be able to distinguish it from your good ideas, from your emotions and impulses, from inspired "charismatic hunches," from other spiritual voices. Go to him as the Master whom you seek to serve. Treat him as someone who always hears you. Be honest. Tell him about the things that confuse you, that frighten you, that overwhelm you. Submit everything to him.

Then listen. You will hear him. His voice will come with that note of "otherness" that will convince you that it comes from God himself.

God did not speak to me very often with this kind of certainty at Harvard. In fact, as I look back, I can see a certain inconsistency in my attitude. On the one hand, a sense that God was calling me to the priesthood grew throughout my Harvard years. This conviction grew in me gradually, more like a seed of truth sprouting and growing than a blinding flash of revelation. On the other hand, I did everything I could to prepare for a successful legal career. I was keeping my options open; I could either surrender fully to God or do what I wanted to do.

The apparent inconsistency didn't bother me, however. It scarcely occurred to me that there was any conflict between my career plans and God's will for my life. When I thought about it, I told myself that the conversation that had begun on Longfellow's lawn had been suspended. I expected to hear more from God about my life. There was always the possibility that he didn't want me to become a priest, I told myself, and if he wanted me to be a lawyer, I had better get my ducks in a row.

Much of the work I did on vacations and in my spare time was good preparation for the priesthood. The summer after the Lord spoke to me on Longfellow's lawn, I worked as a night elevator operator. In summers during college I had worked as a taxi driver, handyman at a women's vacation camp, tennis court manager, golf caddy, and, of course, as a deckhand in the merchant marine. These jobs brought me into contact with working people, blacks, Hispanics, and others whom I rarely saw at Harvard.

I also got a lot of legal experience of the kind law students do not receive in the classroom.

While at Harvard I worked a few hours a week for the Boston Public Defender's office. Our clients were people who could not afford to hire a lawyer to defend them against criminal charges. Most of our clients were poor. Many of them had criminal records. All of them were in jail waiting for trial on serious charges.

The job threw me right into the middle of the realities of the American system of criminal justice. The public defenders were badly overworked; they usually gave the law student assistants complete responsibility for preparing the accused's defense. We would examine the charges, interview the defendant, conduct an investigation if we thought something was wrong, write a report, and brief the defense attorney. Often, the attorney would meet the defendant for the first time a few minutes before the trial and then argue the case equipped with only the report that the law student assistant had written for him.

One day I talked to a garrulous Irishman named Tommy in the city jail who fiercely insisted that he was innocent of the armed robbery he was charged with. I was skeptical. He had a criminal record. I had learned that the jail was full of professional liars when the public defender came around.

But something convinced me this fellow was telling the truth. Perhaps it was his candid admission that he had committed many crimes.

"I ain't no saint," he said, "but I ain't no robber. Somebody else did the job that night."

The problem was that my client had no idea who pulled off the robbery. He had been drinking all day in a bar and had been watching a boxing match along with other patrons the night of the robbery. He woke up in jail. He had been so drunk that he didn't even remember the name of the bar, located a few stores down from where the armed robbery took place.

I went to the bar one night dressed in work clothes and had some beers with the regulars—working-class Irish drinkers who looked and talked a lot like my client. I put on my best Boston Irish brogue and swapped stories for an hour before dropping the name.

"Hey, remember old Tommy? That was some night when he got pinched," I said.

"Yeah, what a loudmouth," one guy said.

"Was he in here Monday?" I asked.

"He wouldn't keep quiet through the Monday night fights."

"Was he yelling when Irish Bob Murphy got the knockout?" I asked.

"He was slobbering all over us," was the response.

That was the exact time of the crime.

I got statements from several witnesses and the judge dropped charges against my client. I am not sure, but I think I know why he was arrested and charged. By the time the police arrived at the bar the night of the robbery, most of the men had fled and those who were left didn't know anything. The cops found my client sitting there, a known criminal with few friends and an abusive way of talking to authorities. They picked him up and charged him.

I was also saddened by what I saw in the neighborhoods where most poor defendants lived. I saw the hopelessness that poverty breeds and encountered the racial hostility that infests our cities. Many people I worked with hated me on sight because I looked like a rich white boy, but I often succeeded in winning their trust and help. A thirst for social justice began to grow in me.

Before my last year of law school, in the summer of 1955, I experienced the other side of the courtroom contest—the prosecutor's side. I worked for three months for the Criminal Division of the U.S. Attorney's Office in New York City.

It was there that I got to know Jean-Pierre Laffite. More precisely, I got to know Laffite's voice on the phone, for I never did set eyes on this notorious spy.

Laffite was a criminal and scoundrel who worked for the U.S. government as a high-level informer in drug cases. Laffite was not his real name; fittingly, he took the name of a nineteenth-century pirate who escaped justice because he helped the American side in the Battle of New Orleans during the War of 1812. Like his namesake, our Laffite was a criminal who became a hero because he gave the U.S. government timely assistance. I never learned much about Laffite. His French accent sounded phony to me over the phone, although it was rumored that he was the only man in history ever to be expelled from the French Foreign Legion for misconduct. I do know that he was not an American. The price for all the information he sold us was United States citizenship. It took a special act of Congress to pay him off.

The last duck to get in a row was admission to the New York State Bar. Even though I had done well at Harvard, I was not ready to practice law anywhere. I had learned much about constitutional law, jurisprudence, and federal statutes; I knew virtually nothing about the laws of the local state that every lawyer needed to know to go into practice. So I rushed from my last law school exam to a special four-week cram course that I hoped would teach me enough about the laws of New York state to allow me to pass the state bar examination.

I took the two-day exam and then entered the Air Force. In July, 1956, I was commissioned as a First Lieutenant. I noted that the results of the bar exam would be out in October—less than four months away.

Work as a military lawyer was difficult and challenging. It was also fun. I liked courtroom work; I was even a bit of a showman. My good legal education, my desire to succeed, and my highly disciplined work habits enabled me to be confident in approaching any legal confrontation.

Judge Advocate lawyers deal with servicemen who are tried in military courts for violations of military rules. Most of the cases are fairly routine. They involve offenses unique to the military, such as being absent without leave and disobeying orders, or crimes that civilians commit as well, such as drunk driving, theft, and fighting. Surprisingly, most of my cases involved attempted murder, rape, grand larceny, homosexual assault, desertion, and other serious charges. I divided my time equally between being a prosecutor and a defense lawyer.

I threw myself into this work with enthusiasm. I prepared my cases meticulously, often staying up late at night to go over my notes or to research possible loopholes in the military law. I tried to come to court better prepared, in better command of the facts of the case, and better acquainted with the law than the opposing counsel. I usually succeeded.

Not surprisingly, I was very successful. In fact, in my first year on the job I never lost a case. The men I prosecuted were always convicted. The men I defended were always acquitted.

In the fall of 1956, I was transferred temporarily from Andrews Air Force Base near Washington, D.C., to Stewart Air Force Base in Newburgh, New York, about fifty miles north of New York City. I was there for several weeks with other Air Force lawyers for special training.

One afternoon just after lunch I returned to the JAG office thinking about the case I was researching. A friend of mine was sitting at a table reading the *New York Times*. He jumped up when he saw me.

"Mike, you made it!"

"Made what?"

"The New York Bar. You're in—fully certified as a Judge Advocate. Look."

He showed me the inside page of the paper where the names of all those who passed the New York Bar exam were listed in small six-point type. There I was: "Scanlan, Michael."

"Let's celebrate," my friend said. "I'll buy the first round at the Officer's Club at 5."

Other Air Force lawyers gathered around to shake my hand and assure me they would be at the party later. I went through the motions of accepting their congratulations, but I really wanted to get out of there as quickly as I could. I was feeling a strong desire to pray. I recalled the agreement I thought I had with the Lord: "I will give my whole life to you, but please wait until I am fully qualified as a lawyer." I was now fully qualified as a lawyer.

I went to my room and fell on my knees. The conversation that began three years earlier was resumed. The Lord was present in power, just as he had been on Longfellow's property in Cambridge, Massachusetts. The conversation was short.

I prayed, "What do you want me to do?"

"I want you to be a priest in a religious order," he said.

"Okay, Lord. Which order?"

But the conversation was over. The Lord did not give me the

name of the religious order he wanted me to join, but he did leave me with an almost military sense of being called into service. I was to be under orders in the army of God just as I was then under orders in the Air Force of the United States.

Later I reflected on the way the disciples had responded to God's call.

Jesus spied Peter and Andrew casting a net into the Sea of Galilee. He said, "Come after me and I will make you fishers of men." They dropped their net and followed him immediately.

He called James and John, who were in their boat. They abandoned their boat and their father and came immediately.

He saw a despised tax collector named Levi sitting at his table and said to him, "Follow me." Levi immediately stood up and became his follower.

I wanted to respond to the Lord that way. I was to be a priest. I didn't know what kind of priest, but I was determined to find out.

FIVE

Francis

I WAS IN AN UNUSUAL SPOT for a young Catholic man who had a vocation to the priesthood. I knew hardly any priests, and I knew virtually nothing about Catholic religious orders.

Since my education in Catholic schools had ended in grammar school, I missed out on the lore of Catholic religious life that most young Catholics pick up in high school and college. I had heard of Jesuits, Benedictines, Dominicans, and Franciscans, but I knew almost nothing about the differences among them. There were large gaps in my Catholic education.

I did not know where to turn for help. Perhaps two priests in the world knew me by name, and both were back at Williams College. My mother and her husband were not close to any priests. I had not gotten to know priests at Harvard or in the Air Force.

I did understand that I was to enter a religious order, not the diocesan clergy. I had once visited a major seminary in the East and asked the rector about the life there. He explained how easy the requirements were—summers off, lots of free time, a weekend a month at home. He seemed to be saying how much the seminary was like the world.

I finally telephoned one of the priests who knew me, Fr. Dan Daly of St. Patrick's Church in Williamstown, Massachusetts, the home of Williams College. He was delighted that I had a vocation and insisted that I look into the Jesuits.

How? I thought when I got back to my quarters that night. I picked up the phone book, found a Jesuit parish, and dialed the number. I made an appointment to come over.

A tall, thin young man dressed in a priest's soutane answered the rectory door.

"Mike Scanlan," I said, extending my hand.

"Welcome, Lieutenant," he said, shaking my hand warmly. "Come in."

He ushered me to a small sitting room where we sized each other up. An Air Force officer and a Jesuit. Two young Irishmen. Two soldiers.

"I appreciate your seeing me so quickly, Father," I began.

"Call me Ed," he said, smiling. "I'm not a priest yet. I am a scholastic—a Jesuit preparing for ordination. I go to Europe for theology next summer, and I hope to be ordained in about three years."

I was startled. Ed looked to be in his late twenties—perhaps a little older than I was—yet he wouldn't be ordained for years. Ed explained that Jesuit training was the longest and most rigorous of any religious order, and that many men were not ordained until their mid-thirties. The rigor of Jesuit training appealed to my disciplined nature. The prospect of waiting ten years or more did not appeal to me at all.

Ed arranged for me to see Avery Dulles, one of the Jesuit order's brightest young priests, now a leading theologian. When I met him at the Jesuit theologate in Woodstock, Maryland, he was already well-known as the Catholic convert son of John Foster Dulles, then the Secretary of State under President Eisenhower.

Fr. Dulles was charming and extremely helpful. He impressed me as a humble man who had submitted his life to the Lord and who took very seriously the possibility that the Lord was calling me to do the same. We talked about my background, my education, my ambitions, my work in the Air Force, and especially about my conviction that God had called me to become a priest. I had never told anyone about my encounters with God in the woods, on Longfellow's lawn, and at Stewart Air Force Base. I told Fr. Dulles. We agreed that I probably had a vocation to a religious order. But which order?

"Why not the Jesuits?" he asked.

Even with my incomplete Catholic education, I knew something of the romance of the Jesuits. Ignatius of Loyola and his spiritual exercises. The battles of the Counter-Reformation. Francis Xavier, Isaac Jogues, and the great missionaries. The worldwide network of Jesuit colleges and universities. I tried to answer the question very honestly.

"The Jesuits are looked upon as an elite. That appeals to me, probably not for all the right reasons. I've always wanted to be the best and to associate with the best. The training is difficult and I like challenges. My call to the priesthood has something military about it, and the Jesuits are the pope's personal soldiers."

"All true," he said, "but other orders are disciplined and effective in God's service. Your vocation needs more discernment."

Then Fr. Dulles said something I knew was from the Lord.

"Mike, a vocation is the restless Spirit of God within you. When that Spirit settles and is at home, stop and join the group where you are."

Fr. Dulles took me over to the Woodstock Library and down to a large room in the second basement. It was full of books, manuscripts, and research materials. A few men sat there on this Sunday afternoon, writing and studying. I suspected that Fr. Dulles would be studying here, too, if I had not come.

"Mike, if you join the Jesuits this could be your life," he said. "Is your spirit at peace here?"

I liked to write and study. But I couldn't see this as my life. This was not my call.

"No, Father," I replied. "I don't think so."

I visited the Dominicans next. The proper name of the

Dominicans is the Order of Preachers. Dominicans had been great evangelists in Europe in the Middle Ages and missionaries in the Western Hemisphere during the Age of Discovery. Today they are mainly known as scholars and teachers. St. Thomas Aquinas, perhaps the greatest theologian of all, was a Dominican. Dominicans had led in the formation of Catholic higher education in Europe and North America.

I went unannounced to the Dominican House of Study at Catholic University in Washington, knocked on the door, and told the man who answered that I wanted to talk to someone about my call to religious life. He was a lay brother. We chatted for a while about Dominican life and how to discern a vocation, but it was soon clear to me that I wasn't called to that order. My spirit did not settle down.

I left as soon as I could after my host made a remark that unsettled me.

"There are two works of God's revelation we can totally depend on," he announced. "The Holy Scriptures and the *Summa Theologiae.*"

By now it was November, and I decided to spend all my spare time learning Latin. I knew I would need a very good command of Latin to get through whatever seminary I entered because most philosophy and theology courses at the time were taught in Latin from Latin texts. I hired a tutor, a graduate student from Catholic University who had left the Franciscan order shortly before final vows. He subtly introduced Franciscan ideals into our conversations about Catholic traditions and history before and after our tutorials.

We often talked about community life. I didn't understand what the life of a religious community would be like, and I was in awe of it. Submitting myself to God was fine. Submitting myself to other men was another matter entirely.

On the other hand, I saw that a religious community could be a great support to a life of obedience and service. It would be a whole new way of life lived with others. The idea of living my religious life on my own did not appeal to me.

I began to see that joining the religious order God wanted me to join might involve a radical break with the kind of person Mike Scanlan was. A will-powered over-achiever like me would find great scope for his talents and faults as a Jesuit or a Dominican. But would I make a good Franciscan? Could I simply obey? Could I obey simply if my life was made up of menial tasks?

My tutor said there was a holy friar right there in Washington, the novice master at the Franciscan house located on the Benedictine property in the northeast quadrant of the city. Talk to him soon, my tutor said.

The next Saturday, I set off to find Fr. James Cleary. My directions took me to a large brick building set next to a boys' academy on a vast estate of ball fields and gardens. This was the Benedictine house. When I inquired about the Franciscans, I was directed to a little broken-down house on a corner of the property. I later learned that it had been a slaughterhouse before being purchased by the Franciscans.

Something about this scene appealed to me. It was incongruous. Was this Air Force lawyer going to learn about serving God from a simple monk living in radical simplicity in the middle of the capital of the most powerful nation on earth? God had spoken to me unexpectedly several times now. I thought this was going to be one of those times.

I rang the doorbell of the oddly shaped house. A young man who looked more like a boy answered, then told me to wait in the doorway while he fetched the novice master. Fr. James appeared, a short man with a big grin on his classic Irish face.

I remember very little about the next sixty minutes because I understood very little of what Fr. James said to me. He was born in Ireland and grew up in Brooklyn. I grew up in Manhattan and had known many Irishmen, but I had never spoken to anyone with Fr. James's unique combination of heavy Irish brogue and thick Brooklyn accent. He also mumbled. I had been studying Latin for three months. I thought I could have had a better conversation with a native

Latin speaker than I had with Fr. James.

We must have discussed monastic life, the Franciscans, and my conviction that I had a vocation. I only remember that it was a difficult conversation and that nothing I heard made me think I should be a Franciscan friar. Fr. James was obviously a holy and generous man, but the inner spirit that Fr. Dulles told me had to be at rest was restless indeed. I couldn't wait to get out of that house.

As I was leaving, Fr. James asked me if I knew anything about St. Francis of Assisi.

"Yes, sure. He's the saint who loved nature. Founder of the Franciscans."

"That's all? Do you know anything else about Francis?"

I tried to recall everything I knew about Francis of Assisi. I remembered his prayer: "Lord, make me an instrument of your peace . . . ."

"Do you have a book on the life of St. Francis?" he mumbled.

I said that I had an Image book on the lives of saints and that one section was on St. Francis.

"Good. Will you read it tonight?"

I said I would and I did. Then I read more about St. Francis. And more. I read as much about this remarkable man as I could find.

Francis enthralled me. The Jesuits and Dominicans didn't suit me because their traditions reinforced my weaknesses. I was too intellectual, too achievement-oriented, too ambitious. I wanted to join a religious order that would change these qualities, not fortify them. No one could be more different from me than Francis of Assisi. The stories of his life had an enormous impact on me.

I read about Francis and the lepers. The young Francis Bernardone was a rich dandy with a secure place in the social world of Assisi. One afternoon he encountered a leper on the road. Nothing disgusted Francis as much as lepers did. This man's rotting flesh, oozing ulcers, and pestilential stench revolted him.

But instead of turning away in horror as he usually did when he saw a leper, Francis embraced the man, and gave him some money. At that moment he felt a great happiness; God was changing bitterness into sweetness. It was a spiritual turning point.

"Ever since," wrote the saint, "everything was so changed for me that what had seemed at first painful and impossible to overcome became easy and pleasant."

I wish that would happen for me, I thought.

I knew that Francis taught the value of poverty. I was amazed to learn that he loved it. I had been raised to regard poverty as a great misfortune that indicated weakness of character. Begging was something that alcoholics and homeless drifters did on the streets of New York. I was astonished to realize how thoroughly, how enthusiastically, and how joyfully the early Franciscans embraced this ideal.

Francis and his little band of early followers often worked as day laborers, as goatherds, as simple carpenters. Above all, they begged. At first Francis was the only one who begged consistently; the others tried to avoid the unpleasant chore. But Francis realized that begging was a spiritual necessity and a great blessing.

"Do not believe that begging is so difficult and humiliating," he told his followers. "You have only to say, 'Charity, for the love of God.' And since, in exchange for what they give you, your benefactors will receive the incomparable blessing of God's love, you will therefore be in the position of someone who offers a hundredfold for one. So be not ashamed, but go forth with joy."

I read about Francis's humility. He quite honestly believed that he was the least of God's servants. One day a bishop who was no fan of Francis made the sarcastic remark that Francis proved that God could draw good out of evil. The fruits of salvation came through such a poor and miserable man, he said. Francis was delighted. "How wisely Your Excellency has spoken," he replied. "You, at least, have given God his due, while leaving me what belongs to me."

Another time, one of the brothers told him that "the whole world is following you, Francis." Francis got down on his knees and repented, saying, "I am the greatest of sinners. If anyone else had received the graces I have received, he would have been much holier than I am."

That struck me. I recalled my first year of law school when I simply tried to be faithful to the modest Lenten disciplines of the church. From this meager gesture had come the greatest of blessings—an encounter with the Lord himself, peace and grace, a direction for my life, a confidence in God, and a conviction that he loved me. How many people had been blessed like this? How little I had done with it. I understood what Francis meant when he said he was the greatest of sinners.

Francis wore rags, lived in hovels, begged in the streets, and lived few days of his life without intense pain. Yet he was one of the happiest people who ever lived. He would make a party wherever he went. Walking down the road with his brother friars, he would take two sticks, pretend they were a fiddle and bow, and sing and dance along.

One day, Brother Leo asked Francis to tell him about perfect joy.

"Brother Leo," he said. "If when we finally get back to our little hut tonight after traveling these many days in the cold and snow, and we knock on the door, and the brother comes out and says, 'Who are you?' and we say, 'We are your brothers, Francis and Leo,' and he says, 'I never heard of you,' and slams the door; and then, Leo, if we knock the second time and we say, 'Don't you recognize us? We're your brothers, Francis and Leo,' and he says, 'No, you are robbers and thieves,' and he slams the door again. And, Leo, if we knock on the door a third time, and he comes out with a stick and beats us and drives us off; if, Brother Leo, we accept all that for the love of God and in union with our crucified Lord, that's perfect joy."

I was completely fascinated with this remarkable man. G.K. Chesterton, one of my favorite writers, begins his biography of Francis by observing that he at first sight appears to be a mass of contradictions. We must try to get a glimmering of why, he said, "the poet who praised his lord the sun, often hid himself in a dark cavern, of why the saint who was so kind to his Brother the Wolf was so harsh to his Brother the Ass (as he nicknamed his own body), of why the troubadour who said that love set his heart on fire separated himself from women, of why the singer who rejoiced in the strength and gaiety of the fire deliberately rolled himself in the snow, of why the song which cries with all the passion of a pagan, 'Praised be God for our Sister, Mother Earth, which brings forth varied fruits and grass and glowing flowers,' ends almost with the words, 'Praised be God for our Sister, the death of the body.'"

The secret of Francis, I came to see, is that he was a lover. He fell in love with Jesus and proceeded to devote his entire life to serving his Lord. He did it in a manly, courageous way that greatly appealed to me. When Francis converted, he was leaving Assisi on a great white horse to seek glory, adventure, and romance in service of a powerful worldly lord.

"Why do you leave the master for the sake of the vassal?" the Lord asked him. He invited Francis to serve the Master of masters, the Lord of lords, and Francis did, with the ideal knight's single-minded generosity and enthusiasm and boldness. Francis fell in love with a King, and he found a Kingdom that was not of this world.

The Kingdom that Francis served was literally not of this world. He understood that the servant of the King of kings had to break completely with the world system. That made him invulnerable. If you took away his food, he fasted. If you took away his lodging, he found perfect joy in the cold and snow. If you abused him and told him he was no good, he agreed with you. If you took away his life, he became a martyr. The world could not force him to compromise.

Francis never had the intention of founding anything. He resisted efforts to give his followers a rule and a structure, saying to those who followed him simply, "Come, and let's live in the Kingdom together." The Bishop of Assisi was appalled when Francis described the kind of life he and his friars would lead: a life without comforts of any kind, without possessions, without any stable sustenance. They would eat whatever they could beg and sleep on the ground. When the bishop suggested that they concede to own a few things, Francis replied, "If we had possessions, then we would need weapons and laws to defend them."

That, I thought, was one of the shrewdest insights any Christian ever had. By renouncing possessions and comforts and weapons and laws, Francis and his followers became free, utterly and completely free. The world had no hold on them. They were completely open to whatever the Lord wanted them to do, to serve him in any way he directed, to minister to the rich and poor alike.

The freedom of the Franciscan way of life itself communicates the core values of the gospel. The gospel says to the world, "There's another way." There is another way for people to relate to each other. There is another way to work. There is another way to treat money and goods. There is another way to treat enemies and strangers. There is another way to be family and another way to be brothers and sisters. Francis found this way—the way of the Kingdom of God. He lived it more fully and more consistently than anyone else. He burned and burned with the fire of the Kingdom—the one kingdom that will last, the one kingdom that is worth giving your life for.

Here I was, as entangled as anyone could be in the world system, struggling to get out but lost in the maze of ambition, success, and pride. Was I supposed to be a priest? Well, I would be a *great* priest, the most successful priest in the United States if not the world. Was I supposed to be in a religious order? I would pick the *best* order—Jesuit, Dominican, whatever. I would do *great* things for the Lord.

Francis was beckoning to me. Or was it the Lord himself? Or both? They were saying, "There's another way, Michael, the way of the Kingdom, the way of the servant." I felt like James and John, the sons of Zebedee, caught in the world's system, entangled in their fishing nets. Then Jesus entered their lives saying, "Come. Follow me." They followed him into a new way of life.

There was no longer any great mystery about what the Lord wanted me to do. It just remained to do it. I decided to become a Franciscan.

SIX

A New Way of Thinking

I KNEW I WAS IN BAD TROUBLE as soon as I drove into the tunnel.

I felt a thumping from the engine through my feet and hands as I drove, then heard a hideous grinding sound. You can't pull off the road in a tunnel on the Pennsylvania Turnpike. I drove on with a prayer. I had gone no more than two hundred yards when I heard a definitive "clunk" and the car slowed to a stop. Trucks and cars roared past in the opposite direction on my left. I looked at the wall of the tunnel no more than ten feet away on my right. I smelled engine oil. I knew that my car, my last cherished possession, had thrown a rod. It would never move on its own power again.

The driver behind me started to honk his horn.

"Get moving," he yelled as I came to his window.

"Friend," I said with a smile, "the way I see it, you have two choices. You can sit here and honk at me, or you can push me out of here."

He pushed. As we slowly covered the remaining mile of the tunnel, I thought how free I was. This was the day when I would enter the Third Order Franciscans at St. Francis Seminary in Loretto, Pennsylvania. All my worldly possessions, a suitcase and a small bundle, were in the back seat of this useless car. I had planned to give the car to my Latin tutor who needed it. Now he would be lucky to sell it for junk.

I thought how well the collapse of my car summed up my situation. I was heading into a new life with nothing left from the old. I had broken with the past. I had burned bridges. The ruined car symbolized the break. It still does. When old desires flare up in my mind, I can usually dismiss them with the thought, "Oh, that's from the days before the car blew up." It was a watershed. I never doubted my vocation after that day. To ask me whether I really wanted to be a Franciscan would be like asking whether I really wanted to be 5 feet 10 inches tall. It was impossible not to be. Why ask?

It was early September, 1957. The previous week had been a time of often wrenching leave-taking. Six days previously I had been suddenly and unexpectedly granted early release from active duty in the Air Force. Senior officers at the base had been insisting that I complete my full two years of active duty—ten more months. The active chief of chaplains himself, the superior of all the chaplains in the Air Force, had reversed them.

This, I was convinced, was an intervention of God and a direct answer to prayer. Young ROTC officers were simply not granted early release from their active duty tours because they had other career plans. Yet I was released and was able to enter seminary a year early.

I hurriedly turned over my cases to other lawyers, processed out, dressed in civilian clothes, packed, and left for New Jersey. As I left Andrews Air Force Base, I had a distinct feeling of leaving behind a whole system of worldly ambitions and relationships that I had struggled with all my life.

In New Jersey, at my mother's home, I had another leave-taking—a painful one—from my mother and her husband. For the first time I told them about my intention to become a priest and a Franciscan.

My mother wept. She would never have grandchildren, she said. I think she grieved not only for the loss of her dreams for her only son's success as a lawyer but also because of her own awkward position as a believing Catholic who was barred from the sacraments because of her irregular marriage.

Her husband Bill was furious. For years he had mocked the Catholic church and had tried to undo my loyalty to it. Now he learned how spectacularly unsuccessful his efforts had been, and he did not take the news well.

Thus I arrived at St. Francis Seminary with the distinct sense of beginning a new life. My family would be new. My work would be new. The values that shaped my thinking would be new. Nevertheless, I felt as if I were finally coming home when I came to the seminary. This was the life God meant me to lead, and he had directly intervened to put me there.

I knew seminary life would be new, but the greatest change I experienced was something I did not expect. My mind was transformed. In Romans, Paul writes, "Do not be conformed to this world but be transformed by the renewal of your mind." This began to happen to me as soon as I entered the Franciscans. The change was far deeper than merely thinking about and studying theology and Scripture instead of military law and political science. It was more a matter of perceiving reality differently, or, more precisely, of becoming aware of a richer reality than any I had previously known.

It was a transformation that St. Francis went through. G.K. Chesterton suggests that Francis's way of perceiving the world was so radically different that we can say that he saw the world upside down. To us, the buildings and roads and trees and machines of our world look massive and permanent. Seen upside down, however, our world looks fragile and helpless—hanging by a thread. According to Chesterton, someone who sees things like Francis did "might see and love every tile on the steep roofs or every bird on the battlements; but he would see them all in a new and divine light of eternal danger and dependence."

I had exactly this experience in the months after entering the Franciscans. I saw familiar things upside down and inside out.

While stationed at Andrews Air Force Base, I had often run errands in Washington, D.C. Some weeks I came into the city nearly every day. The usual reason was to chauffeur visiting colonels and majors to and from the Pentagon. The top brass would come to Andrews from all over the East Coast, ostensibly to review some legal case pending in my jurisdiction but really to have an excuse to get over to the Pentagon. They wanted to find out what was going on, to advance their careers, to lobby for some project or favor, and to increase their power and influence generally. Since I was a lowly lieutenant, I usually got the job of driving the senior officers around the District.

I grew to hate this job. The streets in Washington were confusing enough. But I mainly disliked it because I regarded these errands as distraction from my real work. To me, Washington was deal-making, political gossip, personal backstabbing, looking out for number one, and all the other power games that people came to Washington to play. The day I left the Air Force and drove away from Andrews, I thanked the Lord that I'd never have to drive around Washington again.

Within a year, I was back in Washington for my novitiate in the ramshackle former slaughterhouse where I had met Fr. James. My novice master was Fr. James himself. As soon as he saw me, he gave me a job. Driver.

"You used to work here, didn't you, Brother?" Fr. James said in his Gaelic-Brooklyn brogue. "It's impossible to give people directions in this city. When someone needs to go somewhere, you drive."

So I drove. I drove down the same streets, past the same buildings, on the same highways where I had taken powerful men on errands of worldly power only a year before. Only now the people I drove were humbler and their business was the Lord's work, not man's. I began to see the city the way the Lord saw it, with a transformed mind. I saw it the way Chesterton thought Francis saw—hanging on a thread.

Washington's gleaming white government buildings and foreign embassies epitomized earthly might. The people who worked there affected the lives of people all over the world. Streams of diplomats, businessmen, military officers, journalists, and statesmen from all over the earth converged on this beautiful city to gain favor and wield power.

Yet God held it all in his hand. It was all hanging by a thread. The Washington Monument would topple and all those gleaming buildings would be swept away if God willed it. Washington people thought they were exercising power. The truth is that power belongs to the almighty God, and he will judge accordingly all those who fail to exercise power responsibly. The truth is that Washington is passing away. As I drove around the city delivering mail, picking up visiting friars at Union Station and National Airport, shopping for the novitiate kitchen, I became conscious of being a worker in the only kingdom that will last.

I would see limousines and flags and important men in Washington and say to myself, "Doing the food shopping for the Franciscan novitiate is more important than almost everything else that goes on in this city because that is serving the Kingdom of God."

The education I received during seven years of seminary was a combination of the new grafted onto the old. Priests of my age are among the last to have been trained in the old rigorous style. Vatican Council II occurred while I was in the seminary. Among the many changes the Council called for was a thorough revision of the way priests were trained, including modification of the theology and philosophy curriculum. But the changes did not happen until after I was ordained, and I am glad of it. I think I had the best of both worlds—the freshness and enthusiasm of Vatican II theology building on the strength and depth of classical Catholic theology.

Most of my theology and philosophy texts were in Latin, and three of my courses in the early years of seminary were actually taught in Latin. In my first year of theological studies, I even elected to write an examination in Latin. I grew to love the language for its conciseness and precision. No wonder we studied scholastic theological theses from Latin texts. The English translation often introduced an element of ambiguity and interpretation that was not present in the Latin original.

My steady job was assistant librarian of the seminary. For years my special job was to organize and catalogue the documents of Vatican II as they were translated and released. As I read these documents and the books of the theologians whom the Council had brought into prominence, it became obvious to me that the church I had known would change radically. This did not bother me, although it greatly bothered some of the older priests at the seminary and even some of my contemporaries. I had great confidence in the Holy Spirit's presence in the church. The fact that I did not arrive at St. Francis Seminary through any conventional Catholic channel probably had something to do with my enthusiasm for new things. God's guidance was real to me. Why shouldn't he be able to lead the church as a whole?

Much later I realized that some of the changes ushered into Catholic life after the Council went far beyond the scope and meaning of the Council fathers. They were serious reverses, not gains. We began to take casualties. Under the guidance of the Holy Spirit, I saw that Catholic life in the latter part of the twentieth century involves a battle for the minds of men who are surrounded by ambiguities and half-truths.

In the early 1960s, however, the ferment was stimulating. I read Edward Schilebeeckx and other theologians who became prominent around the time of the Council—on the whole approvingly. These men did not work from the elegant framework of systematic theology that I was learning in the seminary but rather from Scripture and their understanding of human experience. I didn't always agree with them, but I concluded that the prominence they gave Scripture in the theological enterprise was basically sound.

My favorite study of all was Scripture. I was fortunate to have as a professor Fr. Roland Faley, a vibrant and learned scholar who communicated a tremendous enthusiasm for the Bible to all his students. Fr. Roland preceded me as rector of St. Francis Seminary in the 1970s and, after serving as Minister General of our order, is now Executive Secretary of the Major Superiors of Men's Religious Orders in the United States. Fr. Roland taught me how to study Scripture as the word of God, not simply as another text.

Yet the professor who changed me most was Fr. Augustine Donegan. He was the candidate director for the order, and I met him the day I arrived at St. Francis Seminary. He taught me to love prayer above all and to seek all things first in prayer. He opened for me the treasures of a spiritual life, a life with God. He led me to the beginning of contemplation and gave me a thirst for solitude as a place to let the Lord change me.

When Fr. Augustine taught me systematic theology, he linked the love of prayer and the spiritual life with the sacredness of truth. His students learned reverence and awe for the truths about God and his dealings with men. Yet he also taught me to let the Lord change me through the power of the Holy Spirit. This was the bridge between truth and holiness.

My mind was being redeemed.

I was gradually learning to see life the way the Lord saw it—as a battlefield between two kingdoms, as a mysterious gift turned upside down by the gospel, as an arena where the Holy Spirit was active and doing wonderful things. God is at work in the world! The trick is to take the focus off *our* activities and to notice what the Spirit of God is doing.

I am convinced that acquiring this renewed mind is a key to effective ministry in the Kingdom of God. Too often we engage in a "patchwork ministry"—putting patches on holes and band-aids on cuts. We restlessly respond to the needs that present themselves or the work we most like to do without asking what *God* wants done. Most of the time he wants to transform the whole fabric, not patch it up. But we will not know what he wants us to do unless we make a serious effort to get the Lord's mind about the challenges and opportunities that face us.

The mind is usually the last part of our personality to be renewed. Our first confrontation with God is usually an experience of grace—of sheer, merciful, redemptive grace— that has nothing to do with our good deeds or the goodness of our intentions. If we respond to this invitation by asking the Lord into our lives, he will begin to change us. He will put order in our chaotic lives, break patterns of sin, and revolutionize our values. He will point us toward a state in life and give us work to do in his Kingdom. Then he will renew our minds—our sense of what is important, the way we think about life and the world and our relationships.

Sadly, many Christians withhold their minds from the Lord's renewing fire. Paul's comment about the pagans applies to too many of us: "A veil lies over their minds," he said.

If the Lord does not shape our way of thinking, the world will. Our pleasures will be those of the pagans—drugs and alcohol and rock music and the idle entertainments of television. We will view current events the way the media does—as a succession of dramatic crises within a secular political context. Our values will be those of the world— money, sex, and power.

Scripture is very clear on the need to break with the world in our intellects: "Do not be conformed to the passions of your former ignorance"; "Do not love the world or the things in the world"; "Do not be conformed to this world but be transformed by the renewal of your mind."

What *is* a renewed mind? How do renewed and unrenewed intellects differ? A renewed mind is not necessarily one that is trained in philosophy and theology, has mastered Christian doctrine, or can debate effectively with unbelievers. Rather a renewed mind is one that allows a few simple ideas from the gospel to transform its sense of what is important and what is real.

St. Francis had a renewed mind. He grasped the very simple idea that the Kingdom of God is worth devoting one's whole life to because it is the only kingdom that will last. He applied this idea to his life more consistently than almost anyone else before or since. I sensed something of Francis's insight when I realized that doing the food shopping for the novitiate in Washington, D.C., had more importance in the Kingdom of God than almost anything else that went on in that city.

C.S. Lewis, the great British Christian apologist and scholar, regularly astonished his students and friends with his unexpected application of a Christian perspective to "secular" issues. One day a student came into Lewis's room chuckling over an epitaph he had seen on an atheist's tombstone: "Here lies an atheist. All dressed up and nowhere to go." Lewis immediately replied: "I'll bet the atheist wishes *that* were true."

Another time, Lewis and some students were discussing melancholy war poetry from World War I. Most of the poems lamented the tragic deaths of bright young men slaughtered in a senseless war. Lewis suddenly made a remark that put the whole discussion in a different perspective: "None of these poets observes that all the dead would have died later anyway, had there not been a war," he said.

How often have we seized some momentary pleasure or quickly grasped at money or possessions with the thought, "Life is short"? But it isn't short at all. Our lives are eternal. "You've never met a mere mortal," Lewis wrote in one of his essays. "The only people you have ever met are immortals, and they are destined for either heaven or hell." And Lewis points out the eternal significance of our daily actions: "Every contact you make with everyone you meet will help them or hinder them on their journey to heaven," he wrote.

This is true wisdom. C.S. Lewis was a scholar who knew as much about literature as anyone who ever lived, but this immense knowledge did not make him wise. The Lord made him wise by showing him what is truly important in life. Wisdom is not facts or technical knowledge or brilliance or genius. Wisdom is having God's mind. Wisdom comes when his grace transforms the way we think so that he can put our talents and knowledge to good use.

One of the wisest people I have ever known was a young woman named Carol Groves. Carol, a student at the College of Steubenville in the early 1950s before it became a university, suffered from extreme rheumatoid arthritis. She became so crippled that several times her doctors told her that she would never leave her bed. But Carol got up every time and went through four physically painful years at Steubenville getting an education. She had to be carried up every flight of stairs. After she graduated, she served as a librarian at a secondary school for a few years. She was a very holy woman, close to God, and wise. I was honored to be her spiritual director in the closing days of her life.

Carol lost her battle with disease not long after she graduated. The arthritis spread throughout her body. Her hand was amputated. Her body became so fragile that the hospital staff broke one of her bones almost every time they moved her.

On October 3, the night before St. Francis's Day, Carol spoke to the doctors and some friends about the beauty of Francis's life. She also spoke about Sister Death. The next morning she had the nurse dress her in her prettiest gown and make up her face with lipstick and rouge. Then she called the hospital chaplain and said, "Father, could you come up here because I am going to die this morning." He came, gave her the last rites, and she died a few minutes later, a radiant smile on her face. I arrived at her bedside three minutes after she died. I have been present at many deaths, but I never saw so much joy and peace on someone's face at the moment of death as I saw on Carol's.

Carol had a renewed mind. She saw death the way God sees

it, as a small closing and a large opening. "Do not fear those who kill the body but cannot kill the soul," said Jesus. Carol feared those who can kill the soul. She had no fear at all of those who could merely kill her body.

What are you afraid of? Most of us fear sickness and death and the loss of status and friends and possessions. Do we fear these things as much as we fear sin?

What makes you angry? A traffic jam. A parking ticket. An order from your boss that you consider unreasonable. Do you get angry at sin, the things that anger God, things like abortion and pornography, drugs and crime, adultery and fornication? Does false teaching in the church make you as angry as a snub from someone you wish you knew better?

What and whom do you trust? Most people trust themselves and the things they have managed to accumulate. Some people also trust one or two other people—a spouse, a parent, a close friend. But the only one whom we can really trust is God. Only God is wise enough, committed enough, loving enough to be deserving of complete trust.

It's all a matter of seeing the world the way it really is. G.K. Chesterton said that Francis of Assisi, the crazy little poor man who lived in hovels, begged in the streets, and sang the praises of Sister Death, was one of the greatest realists who ever lived. He saw that the world around him was hanging by a thread and passing away before his eyes. He threw in his lot with the kingdom that endures—the Kingdom of God, the body of Christ, the church, the community of men and women who have been reborn in Jesus Christ and who are doing his work. When he came to know Jesus, a veil fell from Francis's eyes and he saw things the way they really are.

Those who have the Lord's mind about the world are constantly surprised. When you renounce the world, you get it all back. The worldly cynic says, "Blessed is he who expects nothing, for he shall not be disappointed." The Christian with a renewed mind says, "Blessed is he who expects nothing for himself, for he shall enjoy everything."

In the seminary I learned to distance myself from the world system. I learned how different the perspective of the gospel is from the perspective that I had been trained to adopt. This was the prerequisite for the surprising work the Lord wanted me to do.

To say the work was surprising is an understatement. When I received my assignment, I was shocked.

SEVEN

Jesus

"GOOD TO SEE YOU, Theophane. Sit down."

I sat and joked a bit with Fr. Kevin, my good friend and superior of my province. I had been looking forward to this meeting for weeks. We were going to discuss my assignment.

I was now Fr. Theophane Scanlan, T.O.R., newly ordained priest in this lovely month of May, 1964. Third Order Franciscans in those days took religious names. I chose Theophane. The name meant "manifestation of God"— something I dearly strived to be. Theophane was also the religious name of my old Latin tutor in Washington, a young man who had been a Third Order seminarian but had left the order before final vows. By choosing his name I was in a sense carrying on the vocation he once thought he had. I was grateful to him for pointing me toward the Franciscan life.

"What shall we do with you, Theophane?" Fr. Kevin said with a smile.

I had an easy relationship with Kevin. We entertained the house often with our political arguments. In this political year of 1964, Kevin would argue the merits of Barry Goldwater while I, a staunch Kennedy Democrat, would urge the brothers to save the Republic from the conservative threat. Kevin and I liked to tease each other and even indulged in an occasional practical joke.

Still, he was my superior. I respected him personally and had confidence in the office. I thought that God's will for my life would be manifest in the decisions Kevin and my other superiors made even if I could not understand them.

Kevin picked up the paper where I had written down my preferences for assignments and peered at it.

"Your first choice is to be a missionary?"

"That's right, Father."

He didn't need to ask. Practically everyone in the order knew about my passion to be a missionary in the Amazon region of Brazil. I had led a mission club at the seminary. I had gotten to know the Franciscans who worked in South America. I wanted to live a holy life completely devoted to the Lord, and I thought missionary work was the most demanding service I could choose.

"I don't think you'd be a very good missionary, Theophane, so why don't we just cross that out?" And Fr. Kevin picked up a pen and did just that. He crossed "missionary" off my list.

I was stunned. Years of striving and praying and dreaming were gone in seconds. Without discussion.

Fr. Kevin looked back at the list. He frowned.

"Your second choice is to get a doctorate in moral theology. The idea would be to come back to the seminary and teach it?"

"That's right, Father. I've done well in theology. I'm sure I could handle the doctoral program. Other people have told me so, too."

"They're right. You probably could handle the doctorate, but we've got other guys who could too," said Fr. Kevin. "So let's cross that one off, too."

He picked up his pen and did it. Just like that.

What's going on here. Where will I be going? I thought.

"Now, Theophane, you probably know that Fr. Bernard, the professor of canon law here, wants me to send you to Rome to get a doctorate in canon law," he said. "Your law degree from Harvard gives you, shall we say, 'interesting' preparation for that."

I did know that. I wasn't as excited about canon law as about theology, but I would do that doctorate if the order wanted me to.

"I've thought about it, but I'm not interested in your doing that," he said. "We'll get someone else for it."

I felt numb, helpless, and apprehensive.

I ran through the possibilities.

He's going to say that he wants me to teach English and math in a high school. I just know it. That's the only thing left. I don't want to do that. Dear Lord, I don't want to do that.

I prayed for the grace to accept the inevitable disappointment that was coming.

"The academic dean position at the College of Steubenville is open. Fr. Columba, the president, thinks you can do it. I'm inclined to agree with him. Do what you have to do to be academic dean of the College of Steubenville."

And then Kevin grinned. As I later told John Sala in the little plane over Ohio, I now understood. The whole thing was a joke. Kevin was up to something else. He was having some fun with me.

But it was no joke. I stared at Kevin, stupefied. I had been in many colleges and universities, but I had never been in a dean's office. What did a dean do?

"Are you willing to do that?" Fr. Kevin asked.

"Yes, Father, but I don't have any idea what a dean does."

"Go to school and find out, Theophane. Go down to Catholic University and take their summer program in higher education administration. If there are other courses you need, take them. I want you to be ready to take over at Steubenville sometime in August." It was early May.

I went back to my room, pulled the dictionary off the shelf, and looked up "dean." "A member of a college or university administration in charge of a school, faculty, special section of students, or of the whole body of students." I was going to be academic dean. I had three months to get ready.

In the mid-sixties, the days before pollution controls, the air in Steubenville, Ohio, was foul. Most residents of the old steel city liked it that way. Air so dirty that you could barely see the huge Weirton steel mill just across the Ohio River in West Virginia meant jobs, paychecks, and prosperity. When the steel mills in the area were belching forth pollutants day and night, families bought new televisions and second cars, they took multiple vacations and talked about college for their children. Clean air meant layoffs, unemployment checks, and a younger generation moving away to California, New York, and Texas in search of better opportunities.

The air in Steubenville has been getting cleaner for the past decade. In the early 1970s, Steubenville had the highest per capita income of any city in the United States. A few years later, when I was serving as president, the steel industry in the Ohio Valley had begun a decline that has turned out to be irreversible. Many antiquated plants in the area are empty; much steel business has gone permanently to Japanese and German competition. Steubenville, Weirton, and Mingo Junction have come to symbolize the decline of America's "smokestack" industries.

The economic decline of Steubenville played a part in the crisis that swept the College of Steubenville in the mid-1970s. Competition for students intensified and low-tuition public universities began to take students away from private schools like Steubenville. The college's location in an economically declining region that few young people found attractive only made matters worse.

In 1964, however, the woes of the college and the city were a decade away. The residents of Steubenville had plenty of money to spend and the college was flourishing in the general boom in higher education in the sixties.

The most urgent task was to bring life and challenge to a dormant academic program. This was my responsibility. I went about the job in my typical style—by stretching my capacity for hard work. I took the cram course in higher education administration that summer at Catholic University, went to several workshops, and read some books about finance, management, and administration. A childhood friend of mine who was teaching at Notre Dame was amused when he found out what I was doing and called me "instant dean." He had a point. I had no experience in college administration and I lacked the PhD that most deans seemed to have, but I liked the challenge and quickly discovered that I could get on top of the job.

My "extracurricular" activities were in many ways more important to me than the task of developing the college's academic program. Everything was happening at once in 1964. As the renewal of Vatican II was implemented, the winds of change started blowing like a gale through the Catholic church in the United States. I decided that I was glad to be dean, at least for now, and not a graduate student in Rome or a missionary in the Amazon. I wanted to be part of everything that was new, and my position as dean gave me the perfect opportunity to do just that.

Ecumenical work came first. The Council's decree on ecumenism spoke very clearly about the common identity that binds all followers of Jesus Christ. It called on Catholics to "recognize the riches of Christ and virtuous works in the lives of others who are bearing witness to Christ, sometimes even to the shedding of their blood." To Catholics who might be reluctant or even afraid to enter meaningful relationships with Protestants, the Council said, "Whatever is truly Christian never conflicts with the genuine interests of the faith; indeed it can always result in a more ample realization of the very mystery of Christ and the church."

I tried to make this ecumenical vision a reality in the Ohio Valley. Ecumenical relationships in the area were about the same as they were everywhere else in the United States—that is, they were virtually nonexistent. Protestants and Catholics worked in the same offices, went to the same high school football games, and read the same newspapers, but they had almost nothing to do with each other *as Christians*. Many had difficulty acknowledging that the others were Christians at all. Cardinal Mercier, the archbishop of Brussels earlier in this century and a great pioneer ecumenist, said that ecumenism begins with contact. "We have to encounter one another in order to know one another," he said. I set out to encounter all the Protestant leaders I could.

I joined ecumenical commissions and boards, preached in Protestant churches, gave retreats to Protestant groups, and encouraged other Catholic leaders in the Ohio Valley to do the same. In 1967, I preached at the service marking the 450th anniversary of Martin Luther's nailing the forty-four theses on the door of Wittenberg Castle. I was the first priest ever to hold membership in the local YMCA (where I often played in volleyball games against other YMCAs). For three years, three other priests from the college and I spent two days a month with local Protestant leaders discussing our differences as well as our areas of agreement. We were the first Catholic priests many of these men of God had ever spoken to.

What did we talk about? We talked about the commitment to Jesus Christ we all shared, about our desire to serve him and his people, and about the practical and personal difficulties we all had as pastors of the church. We talked about our differences. Catholics and Protestants differ on many issues—the role of authority, the place of Mary, sacraments, principles for interpreting Scripture, styles of worship, and many others. The only basis for true ecumenism is a candid acknowledgment that profound differences do exist among Christians.

At the same time, these differences are not as great as many Christians think. Our discussions cleared up some misconceptions. Catholics do not worship Mary and the saints. Protestants *do* have appreciation for Christian tradition. Scripture *is* central in Catholic life. Protestants do not believe that "good works" have no value.

I came to see that many areas of Catholic life that the Protestant Reformation challenged were areas that needed change, or at least renewal. Catholics needed (and still need) a reaffirmation of the importance of preaching the word of God, of the centrality of God's inspired word in Scripture, of the need for personal appropriation of God's saving grace, of the doctrine of justification by faith, of the need for true repentance for sin and not just the sacramental action of absolution. Our discussions also helped Protestant leaders see the value of such "Catholic" ideas as the importance of unity, of authority in the church, the need of both Scripture and tradition, the universality of the church, and the importance of acknowledging and living out a heritage that traces back to the apostles.

Through my ecumenical work I came to realize that some of the most serious differences between Protestants and Catholics are cultural, not doctrinal and theological. They come from prejudices about "Catholic superstition" and "snake-handling holy rollers," ethnic hostility between poor Catholics of Slavic and Southern European descent and poor Protestants from the rural South competing for jobs in the steel mills. Much of the misunderstanding between Catholics and Protestants was exactly the kind of prejudice you would expect between communities that have little contact with each other.

I did my best to establish contact—that vital first step. Cardinal Mercier believed that contact leads to knowledge of one another, knowledge leads to love, and love leads to unity. I believe that we are on the road toward the fulfillment of that vision—the day when all Christians will experience the truth of Paul's words to the Corinthians, "Now you are the body of Christ and individually members of it" (1 Cor 12:27).

Years later, the College of Steubenville gave me an honorary degree for my ecumenical work. Hardly anyone in town thanked me for my other major "extracurricular" activity—support for civil rights. In the mid-1960s, Steubenville, Ohio, was a rigidly segregated city. Blacks lived in a small area downtown; the white establishment kept them there. Realtors would not show a black family a home on LaBelle Hill, Brady, or the West End—the most desirable parts of the city. Blacks who showed an interest in a home in a white neighborhood were harassed and threatened. Banks would not give a mortgage.

I thought that this unofficial racism was very dangerous for the city. Blacks had rioted in Los Angeles, Newark, and other cities in the summer of 1965. Steubenville had just the combination of racial tension, outright racism, simmering black resentment, and rising black expectations that could lead to a conflagration. However, my main motivation was moral. I became a civil rights activist because I thought that racism was wrong. As an official of the College of Steubenville, I was in a position to influence others.

Views were so polarized that the interracial civil rights group split into separate black and white organizations. I was the head of the white group, Concern, but I was also on good terms with the leaders of Combat, the black organization. I had helped Combat's board hire its director, an ordained minister and community organizer named Dick Prosser. Prosser, who had been an assistant to the legendary community organizer Saul Alinsky, liked to call me his spiritual director, a term that poked a little fun at Franciscans, who had spiritual directors, but also accurately reflected the fact that our relationship went beyond the scope of a black-white political alliance. Combat meant business.

On a July morning in 1966, I walked into my office in the college's administration building at about 8:30 and found Prosser and Andy Miller, the mayor of Steubenville, sitting in the waiting room outside my office. They looked grim.

I invited them into my office and asked them what was up. Prosser pointed to the mayor. "Let him tell you," he said.

"Father," Miller said, "we have a bad problem. The blacks say they are going to burn Steubenville down."

Real trouble had come to Steubenville in the same way it had erupted in too many northern cities: Clumsy police handling of a tense situation had touched off violence by frustrated blacks.

The trouble had started in Weirton, West Virginia, just across the river from Steubenville. Steubenville and Weirton are actually one city with the Ohio River flowing down the middle. Incredibly, for a northern state two years after passage of the civil rights bill, the Weirton Community Center had a policy against interracial dancing. The preceding night the manager of the center ejected a young black man for dancing with a young white woman. Angry black youths and others not so young marched down the street to the police station to complain. Nervous police watched the demonstration from inside the station. Then they put on riot gear and rushed into the crowd busting heads. The rest of it followed: looting of stores, random vandalism, arson, wholesale arrests of black youths, angry denunciations of blacks by whites and vice versa.

Rumors made a bad situation much worse. In fact, the rioting that went on in people's minds was much worse than the rioting on the streets of Weirton. It was reported that carloads of blacks armed with rifles were roaming white neighborhoods, that white gangs were looking for blacks to kill, that the police had beaten up little black kids. The latest report had it that black gangs were coming across the river that night to burn down the racist city of Steubenville. People were terrified.

None of this surprised me. Three months before, I had sent the mayor a proposal that he set up a rumor control center to prevent exactly this situation. As I listened to Miller and Prosser, I beat down an impulse to say, "I told you so."

"It sounds bad," I agreed after they had finished. "What can I do to help?"

"We want you to take over the city, Father," the mayor said. His face was grim. He wasn't kidding.

"What did you say?"

"We want you to take over," said Prosser. "Everybody trusts

you, or at least more people trust you than trust the mayor, or the police chief, or me."

The mayor spoke. "Remember that report you sent me about riot situations and rumors? Well, I didn't look at it until last night. It looks good. Why don't you just come downtown and put it into effect?"

It was obvious that the mayor hadn't the foggiest idea of what to do in a riot situation. I did. So I agreed to take over the city for a few days.

I was given a desk with a row of telephones in the City Hall Annex. Mayor Miller told me the building was mine. The mayor, police chief, fire chief, and Dick Prosser all asked me what I wanted them to do.

The first thing I did was to put a black man and a white police officer in every police car in Steubenville. There were no black officers on the force, so I asked Prosser, who had suggested the idea, to find black leaders who were level-headed and respected in the black community.

I set up a rumor control center. People were asked to check out rumors they heard. We promised to get back to them in an hour with the real story.

The most effective move I made was to trample all over the press's sacred constitutional right to gather and report the news as it saw fit, free from interference. I told all the newspaper editors and TV and radio station managers in the area to check with me before reporting anything about violence involving whites and blacks.

"If you don't check with me first," I told each executive, "I will publicly denounce you."

That afternoon, some whites and blacks exchanged taunting words on a streetcorner in Steubenville, then went their way. On one radio station, however, this incident became a brawl between two gangs, and the reporter said that there were reported injuries and property damage. The station hadn't checked with me, so I sent a press release to all media denouncing the station and its management. The newspapers and TV reported the denunciation, and the management of the offending station apologized.

The next evening, a store window was smashed. Other than that, the Steubenville riots never materialized. The young people went home, and their parents in the old Midwest frame houses on the hills overlooking the river put their guns away and went back to watching television in the evenings. After three days on the job I turned the city back to the mayor and police chief and went back to trying to put together a schedule for spring classes that every department at the college could live with. In some ways, that job was tougher than preventing riots.

Steubenville's brush with racial violence brought a lot of people to their senses. The de facto segregation of the city began to reverse. The city and the schools took creative steps to respond to legitimate black grievances. Open expressions of racial hostility became less frequent.

Nevertheless, blacks and whites still live in separate communities in Steubenville, as they do in most northern cities. The races have too little to do with each other. Blacks are still concentrated in the downtown section of the city. Fear and resentment still characterize racial attitudes. Racial division is a social problem that needs our work, prayers, and openness to God's grace.

Four years passed at Steubenville like a blur. I was on the go continually, even recklessly. I would arise at 5:30, celebrate Mass, usually in a local convent, read the daily office, try for a half hour of private prayer, then head for the dean's office and a full day of academic negotiating, planning, and implementing. After dinner, often a hurried meal, I would go to a meeting in town of one of the civil rights or ecumenical groups I was involved in. Weekends I would give retreats, play in tennis tournaments, attend Cursillo workshops, and usually celebrate Mass and hear confessions in one of the outlying parishes. I would try to keep up with my reading while flying to and from conferences. I took a scheduled annual retreat at a Trappist monastery or some similar place. Several times I took an unscheduled retreat for a month suffering from "flu," the word I used to describe that state of physical and mental exhaustion that bordered on collapse.

I tried to keep half a day free every Saturday for solitude and prayer. In decent weather I would take this time in a tree house on the back of the college property that some local kids had outgrown. There I would talk to God and be refreshed in his presence.

Sometimes I would cry out to the Lord to bring order to a life that seemed to be careening out of control. Sometimes I would beg him to change a situation that seemed impervious to my efforts. Most often, however, I stayed pretty much in control of my own life. I would describe my faith at the time as a need-oriented, will-power Christianity that included the elements of a personal relationship with Jesus. The needs would present themselves incessantly—oppressed blacks, poor people, confused students, friends needing counsel, acquaintances needing a speaker, groups needing a retreat, committees needing leadership. I would fill the need, and do it pretty much on my own terms. I was usually confident that *I* could do it.

Yet in my moments of honest assessment, I had to admit that I couldn't do it in many situations. I may have helped avert racial disaster in Steubenville, but blacks and whites still feared and mistrusted each other. The ecumenical work was challenging and necessary, but my efforts to promote interdenominational understanding looked pitifully inadequate in the face of the massive reality of the division of Christendom. Many people came to me for counsel, prayer, and the sacraments with serious personal problems that just didn't change no matter how hard I tried. My prayer would refresh me enough so that I could go back and fight these battles. But for the most part I fought the battles on my own, not through the power of the Holy Spirit.

I was restless in my spirit. Something inside was unfulfilled. I was not the loving, genuine, authentic person I wanted to be. In my relationships, I always had the nagging feeling that people related to me more as a good functionary than as someone to be valued for himself. I thought I knew why. Something inside me resisted love when it was offered and withheld it when it was called for. Everything I did seemed soiled by pride and vanity. In those moments of the most honest self-assessment, I saw that life wasn't these external achievements—being a lawyer, a dean, a theologian, mayor for three days. Life was dealing with God and man in an authentic, open, honest, loving way. Here I had difficulties.

My involvement in the local Cursillo movement helped me to see these weaknesses. "Cursillo," a Spanish word meaning "little course," is an evangelistic movement that centers around a four-day retreat where the basic truths of Christianity are proclaimed and lay people give personal witness to the way the Lord has changed their lives. The purpose of the weekend is to lead Catholics into a personal relationship with Jesus Christ. This relationship is sustained and deepened through regular meetings and ambitious apostolic work.

A member of my order—a priest from Spain—had brought the Cursillo movement from Majorca to the United States. It looked like one of the most promising movements of spiritual renewal to appear in the aftermath of Vatican II. From all reports, the Cursillo had had an astonishing impact on lay people. Lukewarm "Sunday Catholics" would go reluctantly on a Cursillo weekend and return as zealous apologists and enthusiastic parishioners.

The Cursillo I made in May, 1965, changed my relationship with the Lord. I had had a highly developed sense of Jesus as my Master. Like Francis of Assisi, I saw myself as a soldier in Jesus' army, a subordinate under his command. Through the Cursillo experience I began to know Jesus as my brother. I saw that I was *joined* to him intimately, even more intimately than to a flesh and blood brother.

I experienced new power in some familiar passages in the New Testament. "For you have died, and your life is hid with Christ in God," says Paul in Colossians. That meant *me,* Mike Scanlan. *My* life, my life in the Spirit, is in my brother Christ Jesus. That little phrase "in Christ" that appears so often in the New Testament took on new meaning. "I became your father *in Christ Jesus* through the gospel," Paul writes to the Corinthians. That's not just a poetic way of speaking, I realized. Paul really means that. "Have this mind among yourselves, which is yours *in Christ Jesus,*" Paul writes to the Philippians. This suggested to me that many great gifts, including a mind other than the worldly mind we all possess, are ours simply by virtue of being "in Christ."

The most vivid reality that began to penetrate after the Cursillo weekend was the realization that I had millions and millions of brothers and sisters around the world who were joined to me "in Christ." "We, though many, are one body in Christ, and individually members of one another," Paul writes to the Romans. I read and reread the twelfth chapter of Paul's First Letter to the Corinthians where Paul strains to explain the fantastic truth that we are fundamentally one in Christ even though the Lord's people are as diverse as human beings can be. Furthermore, this unity is not a "spiritual" truth but a practical reality. *We are one body, Christ's body, doing his work in the world.*

"There are varieties of gifts, but the same Spirit," Paul writes. "There are varieties of service, but the same Lord." Again: "For just as the body is one and has many members, and all the members of the body, though many, are one body, so it is with Christ. For by one Spirit we were all baptized into one body—Jews or Greeks, slaves or free." And again: "Now you are the body of Christ, and individually members of it."

This vision of unity in Christ spurred me on in my work. In particular, it motivated my ecumenical work. I understood that I had more in common with a black Pentecostal steel-worker with a fifth grade education than I did with some sophisticated, humanist professionals whom I played tennis with in the local tournaments. The Pentecostal and I are members of the same body, baptized by the same Spirit. He and I are brothers.

This simple fact was one of those seminal ideas that fundamentally changed the way I thought about things. My work took on a new significance in my own mind. It was not simply a "good thing" to get to know Protestants and to work together on civil rights projects and other common tasks. It was an urgent priority. This work made a practical reality of the overwhelming theological truth that those who are "in Christ" are Christ's body, doing his work.

Jesus was coming alive in me in a new way. I had known a lot *about* Jesus. Yet now he was coming alive to me in prayer, in my thoughts, in the practical day-to-day details of my work. Jesus was becoming real to me, just as eternal life had become real to me when I faced death in the plane, as faith had become real in the woods outside of Williams College, as vocation had become real when God called me to the priesthood.

Much of what God does in all of us is like that. As he calls us to greater commitment and bestows greater responsibilities and richer blessings, he is showing us how to recover truth and power and riches that lie unused. It's more rediscovery than discovery, more renewal than the start of something new.

This is true in our personal lives and in our work for renewal of the church. We find gifts that have been lost. Through the work of the Spirit, we dig up buried treasure.

Much of the work I did in the city and college during those years had little lasting significance. Citizens for Clean Air (CCA), a civic group I helped launch, epitomizes the futility of much of my energetic activity. The people in CCA wanted to clean up the air in Steubenville, a rather ambitious task. So we talked, read studies, talked some more. About anti-pollution technology. About the peculiar topography of the Ohio Valley. About economic development, and pass-through costs, and labor unions, and legislation, and state-federal enforcement schemes.

What did we do? We printed several thousand bumper stickers and persuaded perhaps a hundred people to put them on their cars. The message was so small that it could be read only when you came close to a stopped car. And when people read the message, they couldn't understand it. CCA did nothing to make Steubenville's air cleaner.

Much of my work was insignificant because I was doing it on my own power, not the power of the Spirit. But it is also true that I had yet to come to the lifetime work that the Lord wanted me to do. I was learning, preparing, getting ready. I had my vocation, but not my ministry.

In 1969, the governing body of our order asked me to become rector of St. Francis Seminary in Loretto, Pennsylvania. The governing body also decided that T.O.R. Franciscans could return to their baptismal names. Thus I recovered my old name of Michael and returned to a familiar place with a new job.

I was a member of the governing body that assigned me to the seminary, and I welcomed the decision. I was ready for something new. The Lord was stirring up my spirit. I liked the idea of being the rector because the job would have greater spiritual content than work in Steubenville.

Something big was going to happen. I suspected that it had something to do with a call to holiness.

EIGHT

Power in the Spirit

H AVE YOU EVER SET OUT ON A NEW JOB, a new city, a new set of relationships, new responsibilities—and felt fear? You began brimming over with confidence, but when the moment actually arrives—when you walk into the new office or when the moving van pulls up to the house—the bottom falls out of your stomach and something like panic sets in.

That happened to me in August, 1969, when I became rector of St. Francis Seminary. As I drove to Loretto, I thought it was a terrific idea for me to become rector. I had participated in the decision, welcomed it, and had no doubt that the Lord wanted me to do this job.

But the first morning, as I knelt in the rear of the seminary chapel and gazed over all the seminarians placed in my care, I felt afraid. I was a pretty good academic administrator, negotiator, committee chairman, and planner. But as I knelt there I knew that God wanted these men to be holy above all else. How poorly equipped I was for this task. My theology studies, as important as they were, did not help me much. I was not an experienced spiritual director, and I was not even sure that wise spiritual direction was the answer. I had had many frustrating experiences in counseling; I knew counseling wasn't the key either.

I tried to quiet the butterflies and look at my situation objectively. A certain amount of uneasiness comes with any new job, I told myself. I was vulnerable to feelings of apprehension. I was an achievement-oriented person. I didn't like to admit that I was not going to be the perfect seminary rector and that I was going to make many mistakes.

All that said, I still knew I was inadequate for this job. I *knew* that I lacked some basic equipment.

I shared my misgivings with the holiest person I knew. She was Sister Caroline, the Superior of the Discalced Carmelite Sisters, a contemplative cloistered community in Loretto. I told her how ill-equipped I was to be holy myself, not to speak of leading others to holiness. I told her about my inability to relate to people in love, about that gnawing, unfulfilled feeling that I had always had.

"You need to be baptized in the Holy Spirit, Michael," she said when I was finished.

"What's that?" I asked. "I've never heard of it."

Sister Caroline told me about her own experience of being baptized in the Spirit. A priest named Francis MacNutt had prayed for her, laying hands on her, and the Lord had done something. It was a mighty work, she said. She felt a new intimacy with the Lord; she *knew* him. She had a new power to love and to minister to others. Above all, she had a new ability to praise God, including the ability to pray in unknown tongues.

I wanted this too. Some of it—particularly the new intimacy with the Lord Jesus—had already begun to happen. I didn't know what to make of this "baptism in the Spirit" experience theologically, but that didn't seem important.

"Please pray with me for this baptism," I asked.

"No, Michael," she answered enigmatically. "You need an expert."

Two experts came in October. Fr. James Ferry, a priest of the Archdiocese of Newark, and Joseph Breault, a graduate student friend of his, came to St. Francis College next door to the seminary to talk about renewal in church life. I was already worn down and frustrated by two hard months as rector. I went to the talk with a sense of high anticipation.

I remember little about what Jim and Joe actually said. They didn't answer the questions of the high-powered seminary professors who were present. The discussion time afterward was full of theological questions, many of which I was better equipped to answer than our visiting experts were. I do recall that I was struck by the way Jim Ferry said the word "Jesus." He said the word many times in his talk. Every time he said it, something leapt inside me. What a strange emphasis he gave to that word, I thought.

After the talk, the theological discussion, and some small group discussion, Jim and Joe said they would be glad to pray with anyone who wished. I wished. I immediately knelt down in the middle of the discussion group and said, "I want to be baptized in the Holy Spirit." Jim, Joe, and Bob Conlin, a seminarian who had already been baptized in the Spirit, laid hands on me. So did some others at Jim's invitation, but in a very tentative manner.

The Spirit fell. It was primarily an experience of prayer, but prayer unlike any other I had experienced or studied. I was lost in God, one with the fullness of life. I wanted nothing more than to know God the way I knew him at that moment, intimately united to him. I let myself go in praise and prayer. God was all I had. He was all I wanted. He was all I needed. I knelt there for many minutes until I was asked to move so the discussion could proceed. I sat in the corner and God immersed me in fire.

Later, when I was asked to join in praying over someone else, I found that I couldn't pray in English. The words came out in some other language. This, I learned, was the mysterious "gift of tongues," the ability to praise God in a prayer language one has never learned. It came to me naturally. I was self-conscious and continued to pray inaudibly but with a new power impelling my words.

That night I went to bed praying and woke up about twelve times—praying every time. Prayer had been going on in me while I slept. I awakened and joined God's prayer in me. In the morning I wrote this sentence down on the pad I kept next to my bed: "I know the presence of the risen Lord Jesus as I have never known it before."

The emphasis was on the word "risen." I knew a lot about the crucified human Jesus—the man who suffered and died, and whose sufferings we share in when we suffer. I had learned quite a lot about this aspect of Jesus over the years as I beat my head against the wall in my work and faced opposition and failure. I knew about Jesus my brother and Jesus the rescuer. But I had known little about the risen and glorified yet present Jesus, the Jesus who governs all creation, who triumphs over every enemy, who carries every burden, who wipes away every tear. Now I did.

I also wrote this sentence on my pad: "I can never deny the truth of what has happened." I knew this experience would not last in its current intensity. I was sure troubles and trials would come in such number that they would threaten to turn the truth of what I was experiencing inside out. I wanted a reminder close at hand.

I was right. I write of this experience many years after it happened. It hasn't always been glorious by any means. People have told me I talked myself into this experience. Prayer has sometimes been difficult, even painful. I have faced obstinate problems that haven't budged at all despite intense prayer. I still sin. I continue to make mistakes. The baptism in the Spirit is a foretaste of eternal life with God, something that hints at what is to come and then diminishes in intensity. I have often referred to the sentence I wrote that morning: "I can never deny the truth of what has happened."

I know the baptism of the Spirit is real because it brought about lasting changes in me. It has also brought about changes in hundreds of men and women I know well enough to be certain that they are different people because of what God has done for them. It is like Paul's matter-of-fact summary of the overwhelming evidence for the truth of the resurrection: "that he was buried, that he was raised on the third day in accordance with the Scriptures, and that he appeared to Cephas, then to the twelve. Then he appeared to more than five hundred brethren at one time, most of whom are still alive, though some have fallen asleep. Then he appeared to James, then to all the apostles. Last of all, as to one untimely born, he appeared to me."

What are these changes? For myself and for many others I know, the first lasting change was in my prayer life. I have always liked prayer. Over the years I have worked very hard at it. I have taken at least a half hour a day for personal prayer and regularly devoted whole days at different times each year to extended personal prayer. Yet being baptized in the Spirit permanently changed my way of praying. Up until that time, *I* had been controlling my prayer time. Afterward, the Lord was running it; the Spirit was praying in me. I learned that living in the power of the Spirit is an experience of being immersed in the life of the Spirit.

I woke up repeatedly the night after I was baptized in the Spirit; each time I discovered I was praying. That sums up the difference. Prayer wells up from inside me now while before prayer was something that I *did*.

I also noticed an immediate difference in the way I read Scripture, a difference that has become permanent. In the days immediately after being baptized in the Spirit, the words seemed to leap off the page when I read Scripture. I reread the New Testament as soon as I could. The words had a new power and seemed to have a personal meaning for me. As I read about the early Christians in Acts and then into the Epistles, I thought, "This is about me. This is what I am experiencing. I know the power of the Holy Spirit like they did. I know where I fit in."

I had been a proficient student of Scripture. I knew how to use commentaries, Bible dictionaries, and other useful scholarly tools. But now the Lord spoke directly to me as I read his word. New meaning in familiar passages was unfolded to me.

I now read Scripture "in the Spirit." I ask the Holy Spirit to work in me as I read and reflect on the Bible, and almost every day I am consciously aware of being led by the Spirit into the infinite depths of God's word.

I also received spiritual gifts. Paul mentions nine spiritual gifts in chapter 12 of 1 Corinthians:

> To one the Spirit gives wisdom in discourse, to another the power to express knowledge. Through the Spirit one receives faith; by the same Spirit another is given the gift of healing, and still another miraculous powers. Prophecy is given to one; to another power to distinguish one spirit from another. One receives the gift of tongues, another that of interpreting tongues. (1 Cor 12:8-10)

I have experienced all these gifts at one time or another, and I have seen others exercise them many times. These gifts are not extensions of human powers but are manifestations of the Holy Spirit, given primarily to equip the community of Christians with all the tools they need to be formed into the body of Christ. These gifts are also given to show the power of God. They help convince us that a divine power is at work within us.

The difference the Spirit makes is the difference between will-power Christianity and Christianity lived in the Spirit. Most of us know what will-power Christianity is. We make a conscious decision to pattern our lives on that of Jesus Christ and to be faithful to his teachings in the midst of suffering and temptations and difficulty. In short, will-power Christianity means using our wills to achieve our ideal of holiness.

The Lord wants us to have a disciplined will, but he also wants us to experience the joy and power of the life of the Spirit. He wants to *do* things for us. He wants us to enjoy the abundance of his mercy. He wants to use us to do miracles. He wants us to know him intimately.

This is what happens when we are baptized in the Spirit.

The experience I had that evening at St. Francis College was real, more real than most "experiences" because it led to lasting changes in my life that I can point to and see. I have listened to many other people describe what it has meant to be baptized in the Spirit, and I know they believe the experience is real, too. Nevertheless, it is not easy to explain this experience. Words tend to make the baptism of the Spirit seem static, a thing that can be defined rather than the dynamic, unpredictable, delightful surprise that it really is.

Two words help, however. They are "empowerment" and "intimacy."

The Holy Spirit empowers. He equips us with gifts and abilities that are not our own. Nowhere is the empowering work of the Spirit clearer than in the Gospel accounts of the Spirit's empowering of Jesus.

The Spirit came upon Jesus when he was baptized in the Jordan:

> When all the people were baptized and Jesus was at prayer after likewise being baptized, the skies opened and the Holy Spirit descended on him in visible form like a dove. A voice from heaven was heard to say, "You are my beloved Son. On you my favor rests."

The power that worked in Jesus' ministry came from the Holy Spirit:

> Jesus, full of the Holy Spirit, then returned from the Jordan and was conducted by the Spirit into the desert.

> When the book of the prophet Isaiah was handed him, he unrolled the scroll and found the passage where it was written, "The Spirit of the Lord is within me, therefore he has anointed me."

One day Jesus was teaching and the power of the Lord made him heal.

He commands the unclean spirits with authority and power, and they leave.

The Pentecost event, where the first believers are filled with power, is described as an outpouring of the Holy Spirit. "All were filled with the Holy Spirit," Luke writes in the Acts of the Apostles. "They began to express themselves in foreign tongues and make bold proclamations as the Spirit prompted them."

Peter later explains: "Exalted at God's right hand he first received the promised Holy Spirit from the Father, then poured the Spirit out on us. This is what you now see and hear."

Peter himself superbly exemplifies the man empowered by the Spirit. In the Gospels we see Peter rushing headlong without thought, speaking rashly, and consistently failing to understand. At the moment of Jesus' arrest, Peter was so frightened that he denied that he even knew his Lord. The Acts of the Apostles portrays a very different Peter—an empowered Peter. He speaks boldly, eloquently, wisely. Challenged by the authorities, he speaks up, "filled with the Holy Spirit." Approached by a lame man for money, Peter promptly heals him. Confronted by the astounding sight of Gentiles praying in tongues, he proclaims the universality of the gospel.

This is the difference the Spirit makes. Power. Power to do easily what before was difficult or impossible. Power to call down God's healing on those who are hurting. Power to face danger with courage. Power to discern the will of the almighty God and to follow him fearlessly.

Power is the visible manifestation of the intimacy we have with God through the Holy Spirit. Intimacy is the second word that helps us understand being baptized in the Spirit. We think and act with God's power after this event because we enter a new relationship of intimacy with each person of the Trinity: Father, Son, and Spirit.

We see the Father as Jesus saw him, as his loving, caring "Abba"—an Aramaic word Jesus used when he prayed that means something like "Dear Father." We come to know Jesus as our brother. We come to know the Spirit as the strengthening, consoling, guiding, dynamic force that we can trust to direct everything in our lives. In short, being baptized in the Spirit means being brought into God's household. We become part of the family. With the Father caring for us, our brother Jesus standing beside us, and the Spirit directing our thoughts and actions, is it any wonder that we can act with power?

Many aspects of the baptism of the Holy Spirit surprised me, but nothing surprised me more than the way it resembled the pattern of God's work in my life. Almost everything the Lord had done with me had the character of a rediscovery of something I had once had or known. The breakthrough of faith at Williams College and the call at Harvard to give my life over to God were related to faith seeds that had been planted years earlier. The same was true of my call to the Franciscans, the renewing of my mind in seminary studies, and my realization through the Cursillo of who Jesus is. It was certainly true of my experience in the little plane, when I finally understood the reality of eternal life.

I was surprised and delighted to realize that being baptized in the Spirit was also a release of something that was locked up inside me.

The graces and gifts that come with being baptized in the Spirit are not necessarily new gifts that come from the outside. They are also the release of graces we have always had, the fruition of a work the Lord began in us when we were baptized—something that happens to most Catholics when we are infants. That is when we are made part of God's household. That is when we receive the Holy Spirit and are brought from death into life. Being baptized in the Holy Spirit is giving ourselves over to the Lord so that his presence and gifts can take over in our lives.

This is a simple step that can be hard to take. It involves a surrender. We must ask the Lord Jesus to take over our lives completely, and we must invite the Holy Spirit in, realizing that we cannot predict or control what the Spirit might do. It means acknowledging that we need something that we are powerless to provide for ourselves. As prideful, self-reliant sinners, we usually resist surrendering our wills and acknowledging our weakness.

But once you give yourself over to the Lord, being baptized in the Spirit is easy. Remember, it is essentially a matter of giving yourself over more fully to the Spirit of God that is already at work in you. It is not something *you* do. It's something God does for you, something he has led you to already and merely wishes to complete.

If you have not been baptized in the Spirit and wish to be, or if you want to recover a fullness of intimacy with God that has faded, turn to him. Do it now. Ask him to release the Holy Spirit in you. Say this prayer:

> Lord Jesus Christ, I want to belong to you from now on. I want to be free from the dominion of darkness and the rule of Satan, and I want to enter into your Kingdom and be part of your people. I will turn away from all sin, and I will avoid everything that leads me to wrongdoing. I ask you to forgive all the sins that I have committed. Come into my heart as my personal Savior and Lord. I offer my life to you, and I promise to obey you as my Lord and Master. I ask you to baptize me in the Holy Spirit.

The prayer is simple. It is a basic commitment to Christ. You cannot pray it too often. If you don't experience God's power, ask the Lord to show you what obstacle is blocking his action. Above all, keep praying.

It's a prayer that will change everything.

NINE

Changes

THE BAPTISM OF THE HOLY SPIRIT brought a multitude of changes in my life. Some I welcomed; some I resisted. But in the end it was irrelevant whether I liked what he was doing. *He* was in charge.

About a month after being baptized in the Spirit, I had an experience that made me realize how firmly in charge the Lord really was and how serious he was about remaking me.

It happened at a Full Gospel Businessmen's meeting in Greensburg, a town not far from Loretto. The Full Gospel association is an international movement of so-called "classical Pentecostals," that is, Protestant Pentecostals from the Assemblies of God and independent Pentecostal fellowships. Catholic Pentecostalism stirred their interest. At their dinner that night, they had two charismatic Catholic priests as guests of honor—myself and Francis MacNutt, a Dominican who had been baptized in the Spirit about two years before me.

When the dinner was over, the master of ceremonies arose and said that Fr. MacNutt and I would pray for anyone who wanted healing. I was shocked. I hadn't agreed to do that. I had never prayed with anyone for healing in the way he meant it and certainly not in a motel banquet room. In fact, I thought that faith healing was usually a psychosomatic release.

But I couldn't escape, so I went to the back of the room. Several people came to me for prayer. I watched Fr. MacNutt out of the corner of my eye and tried to pray as he did—fervently, with eyes closed, and with my hand on the person's head or shoulders. The first three or four asked for spiritual graces and gifts. Then a man stood before me.

"Do you minister healing?" he asked. He was a small man, about forty-five, well dressed.

"No," I said truthfully.

"Do you believe in God's healing power?"

"Yes," I replied.

"Then will you pray for me?"

"Yes, but I don't know whether anything will happen."

The man explained that he was legally deaf. He had just been discharged from his job because of his disability. He said that he thought God had been telling him to have a Catholic priest pray that his hearing would be restored.

"Well then, let's pray," I said.

I asked the Lord to heal the man. I prayed in tongues for a few seconds, then by some inspiration I put my two index fingers in the man's ears.

I suddenly felt warmth, then a tingling sensation like electricity going through my hands and index fingers. The man gave a start and looked at me. He had felt something too. Since then, I have heard people tell about similar experiences of feeling a physical sensation while praying for healing. Inevitably they are delighted. I was frightened. I finished my prayer, said "Amen," and crossed the room to pray for a woman who was waiting for prayer. I didn't understand the electric sensation, didn't know if the man had been healed, and especially didn't like the implications if that man *was* healed. What was I into?

Three months later I was driving through Pittsburgh with one other Franciscan when we suddenly decided to drop in on a charismatic prayer meeting at a monastery in the vicinity. It was a spur-of-the-moment decision, and the meeting was well under way when we arrived. We took seats in back.

No more than three minutes after we arrived, a man stood

up a few rows in front of me and began to talk. He had his back to me, but I heard him perfectly well.

"Three months ago," he said, "I went to a Full Gospel meeting in Greensburg because the Lord said to go. The Lord told me to go there and have a Catholic priest pray for my hearing. I was almost deaf at the time. I was shocked by what the Lord said because I didn't believe that Catholics were Christians. You could almost say I hated Catholics. I frequently told stories mocking priests and sisters."

It was the same man I had prayed with. I was spellbound.

"This priest prayed with me. He said he didn't pray for healing, but he put his fingers in my ears and I felt something like electricity go through them. I could hear again! I went to the doctor a few days later. He said my eardrum, which had been irreparably damaged, was completely new. He had no explanation for it."

The man went on to ask forgiveness for his previous mistrust of Catholics.

I knew that the Lord had a specific reason for having me pray for that man and then bringing me to that prayer meeting to hear about the results of my prayer. He wanted to teach me that things would never be the same again. My life had been unfolding according to my plan for years. Now God was in control. This healing business was something radically new. There would be more radical changes. I had to be prepared to have my life turned inside out as the Lord used me in new ways.

Many things looked the same after that evening in October, 1969. I was still the rector of the seminary. I still prayed in the morning, sorted through a never-ending pile of work in my office, preached, counseled seminarians and fellow priests, drew up budgets, jogged and played tennis as much as I could, read books and wrote letters to friends in the evening, and tried to keep up with many outside interests and commitments.

Inwardly everything was different. I lived in conscious awareness of the power of the Holy Spirit. I knew God was in charge of that part of his Kingdom he had entrusted to my care, and I tried to get in tune with his plan. When I counseled and taught and planned and prayed, even when I jogged and worked on the budget, I tried to be "in the Spirit." I tried to set aside my plans and programs. I saw great results in doing things the Lord's way.

My preaching changed. The Sunday after I was baptized in the Spirit, I preached in chapel to the seminary community as I had done many times before. In the past I rarely received substantive comments about my sermons even though I usually worked for hours on them and thought I usually had something thoughtful and intelligent to say. That Sunday, I simply got up, put aside the homily I had prepared, and spoke extemporaneously with conviction about God's love and goodness and the infinite care he takes for each of our lives.

After Mass several seminarians asked what had happened to me to make my preaching so different. I smiled and told them. They soon became some of the first people that Bob Conlin and I prayed with to be baptized in the Spirit.

Ever since I had arrived at the seminary I had been asking the Lord for clarity and direction about what he wanted me to do as rector. I wanted to ignite a renewal, but I didn't know where to start.

Seminaries were in an upheaval in those days as the church tried to assimilate the changes of Vatican II. Everyone knew that priests had to be trained differently in the future, but everyone had a different theory about what had to change. Some said seminary training had to become more intellectually rigorous and professional. Others said almost the opposite—that future priests should be trained on the job in real pastoral situations. Some experts said that isolated seminaries in rural settings, seminaries like St. Francis, should be closed and that priests should be educated in urban universities. Most thought that curriculum reform was a priority, but there was little agreement on the direction reform should take. More Scripture? More counseling? More pastoral theology? Better training in preaching?

These discussions were more intense at St. Francis than in most seminaries because we trained young men from eighteen dioceses in the United States as well as candidates for our own Franciscan order. Sometimes it seemed to me that every bishop and vocation director we served had a different idea of what we should be doing.

As I talked to these men and reflected on what they said, I became aware of a polarization in the post-Vatican II church that worried me. Many of the older men, many of the bishops among them, seemed to be saying that we should preserve the Catholic world of the 1950s. They liked strong authority, docile priests, nuns, and laypeople, and the symbols of an ethnic Catholic subculture. No one ever came right out and said so, but I am sure that many wished that Vatican II had never happened.

I thought that the old Catholic world was gone for good. Vatican II was meant to equip the church to function in a new pastoral environment, I argued. I was frankly disappointed by the lack of imagination and openness to renewal that many of the church's leaders exhibited.

On the other hand, many younger priests, including many diocesan vocation directors, showed a tolerance for secular and even non-Christian ideas that I thought dangerously naive. I did not think that renewal of seminary life consisted of Rogerian non-directive therapy, Marxist class analysis, sensitivity sessions, and folk Masses.

If the Lord wanted St. Francis seminary to be renewed, he would have to show the way.

In the aftermath of being baptized in the Spirit, I gradually saw the Lord's clear direction. We needed to turn to him. The constant of a young seminarian's life—and of everyone's life for that matter—had to be his personal relationship with the Lord. The rock on which a priest based his life was prayer. Prayer was the key. If the seminarian was growing in the love of the Lord, all would be well with him. If he did not pray, nothing else in his education would be fruitful.

The key to renewal of the institution was the personal spiritual life of the individuals that the institution served. Everything that went on in the seminary—classroom work, liturgy, spiritual direction, even social events—should help the seminarian develop his personal relationship with the Lord.

We stressed the importance of daily personal prayer and developed several ways to help seminarians be faithful to it. One was to emphasize the importance of personal spiritual direction. In the atmosphere of experimentation following the Vatican Council, some seminaries had turned away from the traditional requirement that seminarians have a spiritual director. We did the opposite. Every seminarian had to have a spiritual director whom he met with regularly for counsel about his prayer life.

Another step was more innovative. We asked seminarians to be accountable to each other as well as to their superiors. This was accomplished primarily through regular sharing in small groups. Every seminarian was assigned to a small group. One of the main topics of conversation was their faithfulness to personal prayer. We found that this was a highly effective way to reinforce the habit of daily prayer. The whole seminary community gathered for worship every day for morning and evening prayer and liturgy. We also instituted monthly days of recollection. These communal worship experiences, along with the small groups, did much to combat the isolation and loneliness that too often characterizes seminary life.

I did everything I could to encourage a charismatic renewal of the seminary. Many of the seminarians were baptized in the Spirit in the weeks and months that followed Fr. Ferry's and Joe Breault's visit. I started a charismatic prayer meeting and invited everyone to attend. Many seminarians and faculty did, some regularly. Suddenly, "charismatic spirituality" was a hot topic of conversation around the seminary.

The emphasis on the spiritual life also affected the academic side of seminary life. A new course in ascetical and mystical theology examined charisma from a theological and historical point of view. It was one of the most popular courses in the seminary. We also tried to shift the emphasis in the Scripture department from exegesis to biblical theology. Biblical theology requires a high degree of exegetical skill but focuses on the theology of Scripture rather than on the acquisition of technical abilities to determine what the writers of Scripture intended to say.

These efforts to renew the seminary had mixed results.

The greatest failure had to do with the charismatic prayer meeting. I made a serious mistake by leading the development of the prayer group in such a way that emotionalism came to dominate many personal relationships. People thought that their relationships with each other were based on warmth, empathy, and emotional reinforcement. Relationships based on emotions are relationships that change constantly and never penetrate very deeply. The real foundation for relationships is the objective, never-changing, and unifying fact that we are all brothers and sisters in Jesus Christ.

I ignored warnings from other leaders and continued to emphasize the intimacy of our commitments together. I paid a heavy personal price as I and others became entangled in emotional attachments with the people of the area who attended our open prayer meeting. It took me years to repair the damage this blunder caused.

At the same time, the prayer group bore much good fruit in the lives of many people who attended. It was a place where we learned how to worship in the Spirit, how to exercise spiritual gifts, and how to grow in the spiritual life. The prayer group started many men and women on life-long commitments to service in the church.

We were never able to fully implement the changes in the seminary curriculum that we wanted to make. The classroom side of an academic environment changes slowly. I was particularly frustrated by our inability to recruit the professors we needed to shift the emphasis of our Scripture program from exegesis to biblical theology.

Nevertheless, many individuals made great progress in their personal prayer lives, and the importance of spiritual growth came to characterize the general tone of the seminary. Outside observers noticed it. A team of theologians who evaluated the seminary for accreditation praised us for the vitality and richness of the spiritual life. I was even invited to give a presentation on the subject at the meeting of the American Society of Theological Schools. I know that many of the young men who passed through St. Francis during those years are now faithful and effective priests because they have maintained habits of prayer first developed as seminarians.

In the end, however, we failed. St. Francis Seminary closed in 1978, a victim, primarily, of the catastrophic decline in vocations in the 1970s. The majority of seminarians throughout the years had come from dioceses in the United States that could not train all their own priests. When vocations dwindled, bishops stopped sending their young men to St. Francis and trained them in their own seminaries.

I think the seminary could have survived if it had adopted an explicitly charismatic identity and recruited students who found their priestly vocation through involvement in the worldwide Catholic charismatic renewal. However, the charismatic renewal was too controversial at the time when decisions were being made about the seminary's future.

I still dream of a seminary that emphasizes the power of the Spirit. I *know* that the only basis for priestly training involves building on God's power.

TEN

Repentance

S OMETIMES WE ARE SHOCKED when something simply works the way it should. This was the case with me a few months after I was baptized in the Spirit when I noticed something unusual happening when I heard confessions. People would change! They would suddenly find freedom after struggling with the same problems and confessing the same sins year after year. We would talk and pray, and the penitent would find a whole new depth to his spiritual life.

The theology of the sacrament of penance said this should happen, but I was amazed when it did. Like most Catholics, I had learned not to expect very much from confession. I would listen to people confess the same sins, testify to their power-lessness in the face of temptation, express their sorrow, and I would administer absolution. The grace was given; the sins were forgiven; but rarely did anything more happen. The men and women whose sins had been forgiven would be back the next month or so—to confess the same sins.

During the years after Vatican II, many of them stopped coming back. I was saddened but not terribly surprised to see the dramatic decline in the use of the sacrament of penance. Many Catholics more or less gave up.

Now I was getting letters like these from people whose confessions I had heard:

Little by little I found my fears and anxieties disappearing, not completely, but they were lessening. I fall back but not for long. He picks me right up again. It's grand to feel good and free.

Ever since the afternoon you prayed over me to be healed of all past memories (unpleasant ones) I have been very much at peace. I am a different person: free and so happy I can't believe it sometimes.... I know I have a long way to go, but not even that bothers me as it used to.

I praise the Lord for letting you know my particular problem. Since you prayed for me, I've experienced such a wonderful freedom, and the barrier that I once experienced between him and me is now gone.

When I started to see results like this, I decided to take an aggressive approach to the sacrament of penance. When people came to confession, I told them that the purpose of the sacrament was to effect change. "You shouldn't go back to the same sins," I told them. "You shouldn't be the same after confession as you were before."

After the person confessed his or her sins, we would seek out the root of the person's difficulty. Often this would come to me by direct revelation from the Lord. Sometimes the Lord would reveal it to the penitent. Sometimes we would discern together what the root problem was after discussion. I found that it is usually much easier to get to the roots of sins in the context of confession than in counseling. In counseling or psychotherapy, you are usually talking about symptoms— unhappiness, emotional disturbances, feelings about relationships. In confession, you begin with the more substantive area of relationships to God, family, and associates. Where these relationships have broken down, the cause is usually rooted in sin—the penitent's or another's.

After the person saw how the root problem worked in his or

her life and repented as needed, I would pray for the person. I would pray that he or she be delivered from the work of evil spirits. I would pray for healing. I would pray for strengthening. Then we would make a plan for staying free of sin in the future.

The approach was simple and not very innovative. It looked to me like commonsense pastoral care with the power of the Holy Spirit. But many friends and colleagues thought it revolutionary to think that we should approach the sacrament of penance with the idea of bringing about permanent change. Catholics from New Jersey, Maryland, New York, and other states would make an appointment and drive hundreds of miles to go to confession to me. In 1972, I wrote a little book describing my approach to the sacrament in the hope that other priests would adopt it. Many have, for *The Power in Penance* sold about 180,000 copies through 1985.

This enthusiasm for penance surprised me. Confession is not easy. No one initially likes to confess his sins, especially to another human being, a man whom you know is a sinner himself, with imperfect knowledge of God's will for you. Added to this natural resistance was the widespread uncertainty about traditional Catholic practices that arose in the 1960s and early 1970s. Indeed, while some people were traveling great distances to come to me for confession, American Catholics in general were abandoning the sacrament at an alarming rate. I allowed myself to dream that we might be seeing the beginning of a dramatic revival of penance in the Catholic church.

This has not happened, and the main reason is not pastoral, theological, or administrative.

The fact is that most of us hate to repent. We don't want to face the sin in our lives. We have a weak and incomplete idea of what sin is. We refuse to face the consequences of remaining comfortable with our wrongdoing.

Repentance makes us uncomfortable. We would rather talk about God's love and mercy, the goodness of the Lord, the way the Lord provides for all our needs, the power of the Spirit. All true. But we need to repent as well.

I am convinced that the crucial need for Catholics today is true repentance.

One evening, in the spring of 1985, I picked up a hitchhiker in the middle of town. Preston was a young black man, about twenty-five, who needed a lift for a few miles. But it turned out that Preston needed much more than a ride in a car.

"How's it going?" I asked as we drove off.

"Terrible, man. Everything's down." He went on with a torrent of woes.

"I don't have much money. I can't find steady work in this town. My friends are moving away. I had a woman I wanted to marry, but she just left me. I'm down. I feel bad. Nothing's working."

"What about God?" I asked.

"He isn't working either," Preston said.

Preston had a Christian background, had fallen away, but had lately been trying to come back to church. Some friends had taken him to a few revival meetings, but nothing had happened to him. His friends had told him he was too much into "the world."

"I keep trying to be saved but it doesn't work," he complained. "I'm full of the world and full of these things that pull me down and tear me apart."

Preston seemed to think he could approach the Lord if he could get some of the other things in his life working right. I told him that the Lord had to come first, that nothing else in his life would fall into place until he gave his life over to the only one who could control it.

"But I tried to be saved just last Sunday and it didn't work," he said. I looked over at him. His face was knotted in frustration. He was wringing his hands. When I asked him what he had done, he said, "I prayed with a few other people.

They told me to take Jesus as my Savior. I tried to, but nothing happened."

"Would you like to try again?" I asked.

"Sure. I don't have anywhere else to turn."

I parked the car and prayed with Preston in a way that I had prayed with many people many times before. I led him through a prayer of commitment to Christ and asked the Holy Spirit to lead him and reveal what should be changed in his life. It was all pretty mechanical—until we got to repentance.

I led him through repentance for various sins—for lust, for anger, for cheating, for the ways he had disobeyed God's law. Preston resisted at first, but he became more and more enthusiastic as we went on. By the time we finished, he was a different man. He seemed to be floating in the car. He was laughing, relaxed, happy, free. When he came to taking Jesus Christ as his personal Savior and Lord and asking for the power of the Holy Spirit, he did it with genuine exuberance and desire.

When Preston left my car, he was reborn.

Preston had had many opportunities to give his life over to the Lord. He wanted to do it; he had even tried to do so several times. The difference this time was that he repented. Scripture says, "repent and believe the good news." Preston believed the good news but hadn't repented. He hadn't faced up to his sin, called it sin, and asked the Lord to forgive him. When he finally did, the Lord entered his life.

Some people are burdened with a problem of scrupulosity, but most of us are like Preston. We'd rather avoid the subject of sin. We know the truth with our minds but we'd much rather talk about heaven, the power of the Spirit, healing, and all the other good things the Lord does for us than talk about sin. Our sin.

We don't want to admit that there is something so fundamentally wrong with us that, given a choice between good and evil, chances are we would choose the evil.

But it makes sense that repentance is so important. We can't be saved until we acknowledge that there is something to be saved from. We won't experience the power of God until we realize that we need it, that we cannot live righteously on our own. When we repent and cry out to God, we freely surrender ourselves to God and experience rebirth in Jesus Christ.

Most Catholics I meet need to repent like Preston did. In fact, I think repentance is what most of us need most of all. It is more important than prayer to be baptized in the Spirit. It is more crucial than physical and emotional healing. We need it more than we need the gift of prophecy, or tongues, or the other spiritual gifts.

God won't act in our lives unless we repent. Repentance is the key that unlocks the power of God.

This may surprise you. It surprised me at first, but the evidence that most of us face an urgent need to repent is overwhelming.

During the past fifteen years, I have talked with thousands of Catholics about their personal and spiritual problems. They say that their prayer times are dry, that they are burdened by anxieties and fears, that the work they do for the church is frustrating and unrewarding, or that they despair of ever seeing a particular situation in their life change. These are men and women who consider themselves good Christians and are seeking to follow the Lord and the teachings of the church. Most of them are working very hard at doing the right thing.

Ninety percent of the time, their problem is sin and the answer is repentance. They need to acknowledge sinfulness and turn away from it. If you want to experience more of God's power and mercy and grace, chances are you need to repent.

"God's kindness," wrote Paul, "is meant to lead you to repentance." When the onlookers at Pentecost asked what they needed to do to be saved, Peter answered, "Repent, and believe the good news."

Repentance came first. There must have been many people listening to Peter who would much rather believe the good news than repent. Certainly the world is full of such people today. They say, "give me salvation, give me heaven, give me freedom, solve my problems, and fill my heart with good feelings, but don't talk to me about repentance. That's depressing."

Honest repentance brings us two surprising discoveries: that repentance is not depressing at all, and that it is the key to the joy of the Lord.

Repentance means turning, a turning away from our sin and a turning toward God. It is not a matter of tears and gloomy, grieving feelings about our faults. It is essentially a turning toward the Lord who gives us the grace to repent and to live righteously.

Before we turn, however, we must recognize our sin as sin and acknowledge it as our own. This is the hard part. Something in our fallen nature absolutely hates to take full personal responsibility for sin. People constantly come to me in confession and say something like this:

"I have sinned, Father. I didn't tell the truth about this situation. But of course I lied because I hadn't had much sleep the night before, and the person I was talking to was someone I couldn't trust, and I wasn't expecting them to ask me about it, and before I knew what was happening I had said something that wasn't true."

Or they will confess a sexual sin, making sure that I understand how powerful their sexual feelings are, what terrible trouble they have had controlling them in the past, how overwhelmingly tempting the particular situation was, how they just got carried away, and so on.

Don't make excuses. Don't compromise with sin. When we have done wrong, we are to admit it and take full responsibility for it. We should leave to God the judgment that limits our culpability in particular circumstances.

What is sin? Most of us memorize the ten commandments in school: We are not to kill, not to commit adultery, not to steal what belongs to someone else, to honor our parents, and so on. But how many of us memorize the Lord Jesus' comments about these laws in the New Testament? Look at the fifth chapter of Matthew's Gospel:

"You have heard that it was said to the men of old, 'You shall not kill; and whoever kills shall be liable to judgment.' But I say to you that everyone who is angry with his brother shall be liable to judgment; whoever insults his brother shall be liable to the council, and whoever says 'You fool!' shall be liable to the hell of fire."

"You have heard that it was said, 'You shall not commit adultery.' But I say to you that every one who looks at a woman lustfully has already committed adultery with her in his heart."

"You have heard that it was said, 'An eye for an eye and a tooth for a tooth.' But I say to you, Do not resist one who is evil. But if any one strikes you on the right cheek, turn to him the other also."

"You have heard that it was said, 'You shall love your neighbor and hate your enemy.' But I say to you, Love your enemies and pray for those that persecute you."

"You, therefore, must be perfect, as your heavenly Father is perfect."

These passages seldom rank high on our lists of favorite New Testament teachings. Jesus seems to be setting forth an unattainable standard. How can we measure up to such strict ideals?

Part of what Jesus is saying here, I think, is something like "Be honest and stop kidding yourself." The question is not "have I avoided doing wrong according to the law?" but rather "where is my heart?" If you refrain from killing but are still seething with anger and resentment, you are legally innocent but spiritually guilty. If you avoid the act of adultery but give in to adulterous fantasies and longings, how righteous *are* you? If you stay out of jail but wish evil on everyone who does you wrong, how are you living the life of the Lord, who died to save miserable sinners who hated him?

The truth is that these thoughts and actions and decisions are sinful. Stop telling yourself lies and making fancy rationalizations, Jesus says. You *know* they are sinful.

A key to this passage in Matthew 5 is verses 29-30:

> "If your right eye causes you to sin, pluck it out and throw it away; it is better that you lose one of your members than that your whole body be thrown into hell. And if your right hand causes you to sin, cut it off and throw it away; it is better that you lose one of your members than that your whole body go into hell."

Of course it's better! Who would question that it is better to lose eyes, hands, feet, even earthly life itself, than to lose eternal life with God? This is exactly what Jesus means when he points to our inner motives, to the lust in our hearts, to the secret passions and unspoken resentments that we so carefully hide from the world, even from ourselves. He is saying: break with whatever tends toward sin and away from me.

In the world's eyes, Matthew 5 is a foolish teaching. Pluck out your eye! Cut off your hand! Our world adeptly turns sin into virtue. What Scripture calls pride and rebellion our culture calls "doing your own thing," "doing what I want with my body," "fulfilling myself," and "looking out for number one." What the Lord calls killing the world calls "euthanasia," "terminating pregnancy," "compassionate release," and "disposing of the products of conception."

Nowhere is the ugly nature of sin hidden more adroitly than in the gigantic hoax that is the so-called sexual revolution. Once, while reading a magazine article on contemporary sexual behavior, I made a list of the words used to describe the sins of fornication, adultery, and homosexuality. They include: having an affair, sleeping together, going to bed, having a serious relationship, an open marriage, a trial marriage, making love, a one-night stand, living together, common quarters, affectionate roommates, gay sex, alternative life-styles, swinging, bi-sexual, and pan-sexual. The last term was a new one for me. I gather that "pan-sexual" means people who take their sex anywhere they can get it.

These are the words used to describe a free and sophisti-cated lifestyle, the open flaunting of God's law that mas-querades as the cool, liberated way to live. We see the prophecy in George Orwell's *1984*. In that novel, the mission of the Propaganda Department, which was called the Ministry of Truth, was to spread lies by turning language inside out. War is peace, it declared. Hate is love. In our world, sin is virtue and the righteous are wrong.

Christians often talk about how difficult it is to survive in today's world. I suspect that the values of society have *always* been a danger to Christians. In the first, the tenth, or the twentieth centuries, Christians have *always* been in trouble if they accept the world's values over the Bible's. Our propa-ganda machine may be the most ubiquitous in human history, but the truth is that we *never* want to look honestly at our sin. There have *always* been people who will tell us that we have nothing to worry about.

One of my ministries has been to preach repentance—to tell people that there *is* something to worry about. This is a message that lies at the heart of my Franciscan vocation, and which I have preached with ever-increasing urgency in the Catholic evangelistic alliance known as FIRE.

Repentance was the word that St. Francis of Assisi preached to the men and women of the thirteenth century. My own order, the Third Order Regular of St. Francis of Penance, originated in the lay people who wanted to be counted among

Francis's faithful followers because they responded to his call to repentance and holiness. Francis understood the seductiveness of the world's lures and the infinite human capacity for self-deception better than almost anyone who ever lived. The weapon he used to battle the evil of the thirteenth century was a call to repentance. He did public penance himself to show what he meant. The Franciscan habit, the familiar garb of Francis's followers for more than 800 years, is the dress of sinners making a public statement of their sorrow for their offenses.

We smile at cartoons of religious fanatics carrying signs saying "Repent!" But that's precisely what Francis did in medieval Europe and that's what his followers do today.

This is what I do in the FIRE alliance.

FIRE is an evangelistic Catholic alliance that seeks to lead people to an initial, renewed, or deeper conversion. The four letters of the name FIRE stand for the four components of its message: faith, intercession, repentance, and evangelism. Faith is the gift that allows us to see the fallen condition of the world clearly and embrace the way to salvation. Intercession is the weapon we use to change the misery we see around us. Repentance is the essential turning to the Lord that unlocks the power of prayer and the Holy Spirit. Evangelism is the goal—the commitment to spread the word and turn ever more deeply to our Savior.

FIRE is an alliance in two senses. It brings together four Catholic leaders—Ralph Martin, Ann Shields, Fr. John Bertolucci, and myself—who seek to preach a united message. FIRE is also an alliance of everyone who wants to stand together in a commitment to personal prayer, intercession, repentance, and evangelism. We are motivated by the words of Jesus: "I have come to cast fire on the earth; and would that it were already kindled."

My particular role in FIRE has been to preach about repentance. I do it in my Franciscan habit, in continuity with the founder of my order. I believe that repentance lights the fire of God in people's lives and releases the power of the Holy Spirit. I have seen it happen numerous times, as I am sure Francis did.

I preach about deceit. We need to heed the word of Paul in Ephesians: "Put off your old nature which belongs to your former manner of life and is corrupt through deceitful lusts, and be renewed in the spirit of your minds, and put on the new nature, created after the likeness of God in true righteousness and holiness."

"Deceitful lusts" perfectly describes our problem. Our desires blind us. We lust after all manner of things—money and people, travel, food, stereo systems, homes, honor and riches, acclaim and love. But these goods of the world deceive us. They obscure from us the fact that our true fulfillment lies in God, and that pursuing the things of the world draws us farther and farther away from him.

Our lusts also deceive us about our actions. As we chase money, sex, and power, we tell ourselves that this is life, that reality forces us to make the nasty compromises and ugly decisions that cause us to lie awake nights and feel ashamed when we come to the Lord in prayer. The Lord is saying that these compromises are wrong, that we must see them for what they are. As sins.

Once we admit the sin, we must turn away from it. This can be very difficult. Often the sin is a habit. Very often we have to admit that we *like* the sin. We are comfortable with our anger, our resentment, our lust, our craving for success and honor. Think about this honestly. How often have you faced a decision to turn away from something that you know is wrong, but have had terrible trouble actually *doing it*? Your brain told you that the relationship, the substance, the emotion was wrong, but something within you fiercely resisted the step of actually putting it aside. "For I do not do the good I want, but the evil I do not want is what I do," wrote an anguished Paul. He continued: "Who will deliver me from this body of death?

Thanks be to God through Jesus Christ our Lord."

Jesus will deliver you from your unruly passions, your selfishness, your unfaithfulness, your self-deception. Just ask him to do it. Don't wait for intense feelings of remorse and regret to motivate you; they may never come. Don't wait for a time when you are ready to give up your sin; you may never "want" to. If you are comfortable with your sin and feel powerless before it, tell the Lord. Ask him for the power to change. Throw yourself before the source of mercy.

And then change. Take the grace the Lord gives and simply turn away from your sin and turn toward the Lord in holiness.

As you do this, you will discover the secret about repentance that Christians throughout the ages have learned. This is that repentance leads to joy. Repentance is not sad. Sin is sad. When we repent and put sin behind us, the time for rejoicing has come.

Joy isn't a feeling we can conjure up at will. Rather it is a response to a life being lived the way God wants it, a holy life free of sin.

You were made for God. He is the one who will set your heart at rest and fulfill your deepest longings. He is the only one who is sufficient to meet all your needs. Sin is what separates you from him. Repentance is what removes the barriers and brings you into closer union with him. The natural response when this happens, the excitement that wells up from inside, is joy. For a Christian whose sins are forgiven and who lives in Christ, it really is possible to rejoice always.

One evening ten years after I had become president of the University of Steubenville, I found myself violently, helplessly sick in a motel in Hamilton, Ohio. I was there alone on a fund-raising errand and was suddenly laid low the evening my business was concluded. I lay in my bed with fever, chills, vomiting, diarrhea, headache, and all the rest of the misery of a violent attack of flu. I was so miserable that I wondered whether I would leave the motel alive. I even started to think that I would welcome a speedy death.

Then a small voice in my mind said to me, "Michael, you can praise me even now."

And it was true. I could praise the Lord even in the midst of my loneliness and physical misery. In a certain sense it was easier to rejoice in the Lord in those circumstances because it was easier to see that the Lord was all I had.

"Am I sufficient for you, Michael?" the Lord asked.

He was. It was a moment when I could see the real nature of the relationship between us. I had absolutely nothing to offer the Lord except my helplessness and suffering. I was at my absolutely lowest point. And yet—God was there. The Father was my Father, Jesus was my brother, and the power of the Holy Spirit was available to me. I decided to use a little of that power. I praised the Lord. I rejoiced above all that I was able to recognize that he was sufficient.

Repentance is the key to this relationship. It brings us from the twilight into the light of truth.

Our inclination is to live as children of the twilight. Given our ordinary human instincts, we try to get away with as much as we can. We ask ourselves how far we can go without sinning. So we fool around with sinful situations and sinful companions, we entertain sinful thoughts and desires there in the twilight, and more often than not we end up sinning.

Is it any wonder that we lack joy, that we complain about being frustrated and anxious, unfulfilled and burdened with cares and worries?

The answer is the one given by John the Baptist, Jesus, and Peter when people asked them for help.

Repent.

ELEVEN

Healing

R EPENTANCE IS THE ESSENTIAL FIRST STEP in building, rebuilding, or renewing our relationship with the Lord. Repentance means death—death to our flesh, to our human resourcefulness, to our sins. Out of this death comes life—new life in Jesus and new power in the Holy Spirit.

A second step is healing. When Jesus is Lord of our lives, he reveals himself as a healer.

Revelation often hits me when I am ill. It probably has something to do with being in a position where I *know* that I am weak and need the Lord, something I tend to forget when I am well.

This revelation happened one frigid January afternoon in 1971. I had returned to the seminary from a conference in Ann Arbor. Hong Kong flu had swept through the Ann Arbor assembly like one of the plagues of Egypt. Most of the speakers at the conference, including speakers who had led healing workshops, had been struck down. I had a particularly severe case. I had actually checked into the hospital in Ann Arbor because I was showing signs of malaria, apparently contracted five months earlier in the Amazon. After a few more days of rest in Michigan, I managed to get on a plane and returned home, still very ill.

About an hour after I got home, I was lying face down on my bed trying to get up enough strength to change into my pajamas when I heard a knock on my door. It was a seminarian. He jumped into the room on one foot.

"Father Mike, my foot's broken," he said as he slumped into a chair. "I'm sure of it. I was playing volleyball. I went up for a block, came down on the side of my foot, and I heard it crack."

I looked at him with half-closed eyes. Did he want my permission to go to the hospital? I had never been so sick in my life. I couldn't move. I felt bad for him, but I felt worse for myself.

"Could you pray with me, Father?" he asked.

Was he kidding? Some people around the seminary made little jokes about the charismatic revival that had been going on. But this young man wasn't one of them. I decided that he was serious. He really wanted the deathly ill rector to pray for his foot.

"I can't get up, Bill," I said. "Bring your foot over here."

He dragged his chair across the floor and put his foot in my face. I raised my arm, and put it on the swollen foot.

"Jesus, please heal Bill's foot," I croaked.

That was all I could say or do. I couldn't hold my arm up any more and I couldn't talk. But, as it turned out, that was all I needed to do.

Bill said "look" and about thirty seconds later he was bounding around the room. "It's healed. My foot's healed. Father, you healed my foot." He ran out of the room and down the corridor, yelling, "Come look at this, brothers, my foot was broken, but Father Mike healed it."

I lay there in bodily misery but in spiritual fever. "*I* didn't heal him, Lord, but you did," I said. "Why did it work so simply?"

I reflected. Of course, the Lord healed Bill because he loved him, but I thought there was a message for me in that healing too. I had been struggling to overcome my pride and vanity for many years. Perhaps the Lord wanted to work through me at a time when there was no doubt that *he* was the one who was acting.

But there was more. Later, when I had recovered a little, I reached for my Bible and prayed for a passage. My hand fell on Acts 4:29. The passage described the great thanksgiving of the Jerusalem church after the authorities released Peter and John. In this time of persecution and great trial, the people prayed: "Lord, look upon their threats, and grant to thy servants to speak thy word with all boldness, while thou stretchest out thy hand to heal, and signs and wonders are performed through the name of thy holy servant Jesus."

This is, I realized, a time of visitation. Our time is an era of accelerating evil and great pressure on the church. It is also a time when God is working with great power, when his graces are available in an abundance and with a kind of public exposure that is without precedent.

Healing is a major part of this public display of God's power. But healing is not to be cherished in itself. It points toward the Lord Jesus, and then to the Lord's plan for our time.

The story of my involvement in the healing ministry is the story of learning how healing both embodies and points toward the larger thing God is doing among us. It is a story of God's great, merciful love and my weakness.

The basic lesson I learned in the healing ministry is that God is way ahead of us. The Lord taught me this in an almost embarrassing way when I was virtually dragged into praying with the deaf man at the Full Gospel Businessmen's dinner. But the Lord keeps teaching us that his graces are far more abundant than we think. He wants to do much more than we expect him to, in ways that we cannot even dream of. We put God in a box. He won't be limited in any way.

One afternoon while walking through the lobby of a hotel in Grand Rapids, Michigan, I became aware of a disturbance in one corner of the room. I walked in that direction, in that casual way we use to check out disturbances in public places without announcing our curiosity. A boy of about four was screaming and rolling around on the floor in some kind of a fit.

Several people were trying to help the parents control the child. A crowd was gathering. It was a bad situation.

Then the Lord spoke to me.

"I want you to pray with that boy for a complete healing," he said. It wasn't an audible voice. But I "heard" the Lord say this as clearly as I have ever heard anything.

I suspected that the boy had Down's Syndrome. I was astonished. Down's Syndrome is a genetic defect that always causes moderate to severe mental impairment and physical disability. Every cell in that boy's body had an extra chromosome. Every one of the billions of cells in his body was defective, and I was supposed to pray for a complete healing.

But I had heard the Lord. I took a deep and uneasy breath, went over to the parents, and said that I wanted to pray for their son. I wanted to imply that the idea was mine, not the Lord's, in case nothing happened when I prayed.

I put my hands on the child and prayed. He calmed down immediately. I was filled with a sense that at that moment the Lord began to restore him completely.

He was. In the weeks and months following that event, the boy's development accelerated. The doctors could not find any explanation for it. When they ran tests they could find no trace of Down's Syndrome. I still hear from the parents telling me how well he is doing.

A miracle? Probably. God made whole what sin and Satan had twisted. It is a foretaste of the wholeness we will all experience when we are in heaven with the Father, Son, and Spirit. And the Lord's ideas of how this will happen on earth are far greater than ours.

A few years after I was baptized in the Spirit, I baptized my half-brother's daughter, Darlene. A few months later I was visiting my brother and his wife. They told me some bad news: my niece Darlene was deaf.

"She doesn't hear anything," my brother said. Many doctors had examined her, but none of them gave any hope that she would ever hear.

During that visit, I slipped into Darlene's room where she was sleeping. I was overcome with God's love for her. I anointed her with oil, laid my hands on her head, and felt God's power rush through my hands.

Three days later, my brother slammed Darlene's bedroom door while she was sleeping. She cried. Tests a few days later confirmed the remarkable fact: God had healed her. Darlene's hearing was normal. I have told this story frequently because this healing communicates God's personal love more powerfully than the others; it happened in my family.

These experiences, which occurred shortly after I was baptized in the Spirit, taught me several lessons about how I was to use this new power available in the body of Christ. I think they are lessons for all of us.

First, I have made it a habit to pray for healing whenever a need presents itself. If a student at the university tells me he is ill, I pray with him or her. If someone I am visiting complains of a physical or even an emotional or psychological problem, I suggest that we pray. I have even prayed with people over the phone. The Lord has made it clear to me that I cannot judge when and how he might want to heal someone.

I don't know what is going to happen when I pray with someone. Some people are healed on the spot. Some are healed later. Sometimes the physical problem remains but the person experiences a spiritual or emotional healing. Sometimes nothing seems to happen. Sometimes people are healed before I can get around to praying for them.

The watchword is: pray! *You* may not know what the Lord wants to do. But you can be certain that his intentions are larger than yours.

The other lesson I learned in my early experiences of healing is to listen carefully to the Lord. Kathryn Kuhlman, the great Pentecostal evangelist, used to say that she never healed anybody or even had a ministry of healing. All she did was listen to the Lord tell her whom he was healing and ask those people to come up to be blessed and give testimony.

I learned this lesson in the most personal way possible. It happened to me.

All my life I had suffered from allergies. I was three years old when I began getting injections to control the sneezing, headaches, and asthmatic breathing that plagued my life. The problem was so bad that my superiors in the Air Force sent me to Walter Reed Naval Hospital for special diagnostic tests. The allergists discovered that I was seriously allergic to 85 different substances—more than anyone they had ever tested. Dog hair was the substance I was most sensitive to. If I walked into a house where a dog lived, I would be sneezing and wheezing within minutes.

After being baptized in the Spirit, I began going to Kathryn Kuhlman healing services in Pittsburgh whenever I could. The third time I attended I stopped at the healing service a few hours before a scheduled appointment with my allergist. During the service Kathryn announced that the Lord was healing a man who had allergies, and she proceeded to describe someone with my exact symptoms. I didn't notice any change. Later, she came down the aisle and laid her hands on me saying, "The glory of God is on this man." I experienced great power and fell to the floor.

A few hours later, my body rejected the serum injected by the doctor. Immediately that day, I noticed an immunity to many substances which had been serious causes of hayfever and asthma.

The healing has persisted. It has not been a complete healing. I am still bothered from time to time by dog hair and other foods and substances. But it has been a massive healing that I cannot doubt is real.

Since then I have always tried to follow Kathryn Kuhlman's advice to discern what the Lord is doing in healing. When I pray for healing under a genuine impulse of God-given expectant faith, I always see something tangible happen. The expectant faith is something the Lord gives. He doesn't always give it, at least as far as I am able to discern. I suspect that the Lord always gives direction in how to pray in every healing situation; I am just limited in my ability to hear him.

I do know this: when I hear the Lord, I see results.

I put this principle into practice for the first time at a charismatic renewal conference in Trinidad in the mid-1970s. Much to my surprise (and annoyance) the conference chairman announced at the end of the evening session that I would lead a healing session the next afternoon. She hadn't consulted me. This was during the time that I was still very uneasy about having a healing ministry.

I went over to the pool and swam lap after lap and asked the Lord how to run a healing workshop. I had never done such a thing alone before.

"Do what John the Baptist did," he said.

"What was that, Lord?" I asked.

"He pointed toward *me*: 'Behold the Lamb of God.'"

That afternoon wonder upon wonder cascaded down upon the healing workshop. All I did was pray and point out what the Lord was doing. What he was doing was healing people— healing them of asthma and poor backs, of deafness and poor eyesight, of respiratory diseases and twisted limbs. It was magnificent. All I did was stand back and announce what God was doing. It was all God's work.

I dislike the term "faith-healing" because it suggests that something other than the Lord's sovereign and mysterious grace is at work in healing, but it does point out something that is true. A key element in healing is faith. Healing is almost always associated with *someone's* faith—the faith of the sick person; the faith of the minister; the faith of the assembly.

When I prayed for my niece's deafness, I was filled with an absolute certainty that the Lord was going to heal her. When I anointed her ears with oil, I *knew* the Lord had done something through my action to heal her. When my brother called to say that the doctors had tested her hearing as normal, I was delighted, but not surprised. He confirmed something I knew was going to happen.

I have this kind of faith-filled certainty of healing about twenty percent of the time I pray. This kind of faith is the basis of healing ministries by Sr. Briege McKenna, Kathryn Kuhlman, John Wimber, and others. God gives them more faith than he gives to most of us who pray for healing. I think this faith consists of a special sensitivity to what the Lord is doing by way of healing.

Other times, the gift of faith is given to the one who needs healing. This was clearly the case when I prayed for the deaf man at the Full Gospel dinner. I didn't know what I was doing; all I wanted to do was to get out of the room. But the man was firmly convinced that God wanted him to be prayed with for healing by a Catholic priest, and he had enough faith to obey despite his prejudice against Catholics. He was like the woman who touched the hem of Jesus' garment and was healed, or the Roman centurion whose servant Jesus cured with the comment, "I have never found so much faith among the Israelites."

Sometimes God gives the gift of faith for healing to other believers—friends of the sick person, associates of the one praying for healing, or the congregation as a whole. This seems to be the case with the healing of the paralytic man at Capernaum. The man could not get close to Jesus because of the crowds. The paralytic's friends, determined to see him healed, took him up to the roof of the house where Jesus was staying and lowered him by rope to Jesus' feet. The Scripture says that Jesus acted "when he saw *their* faith."

I have been present at healing gatherings where the assembly itself seemed to be saturated with faith for healing, and the healings came in abundance. I have often seen people healed when neither they nor the people praying with them had any special faith for healing, but a spouse, parent, or close friend did.

Healing is also closely associated with intercession. In fact, healing is connected to the intercessory prayer of the church—the daily liturgies, the prayers of monks in the cloister and of busy homemakers and business people, the intercessory prayers of people like you and me.

We at the University of Steubenville saw the dramatic truth of this one evening when Fr. Ed Wade, a priest associated with us, led what he called a festival of praise in the college chapel. The students praised the Lord for a few hours; then Fr. Wade led the congregation in intercessory prayer for healing. The students were spontaneously healed of all kinds of illnesses and problems, ranging from nagging coughs and tension headaches to hearing loss and a crippled arm.

Before you pray for healing, pray for faith. Pray for a charismatic faith, a faith that is infused and certain. Pray for a certain knowledge of what the Lord wants to do in any situation involving healing. When a person who is sick or crippled or dying stands before you and asks for prayer, you first pray in faith and ask the Lord what he wants to do.

If God impresses on you the sense that the person will be healed, and you are sure it is God, then stand firmly on that word in faith. Do not be afraid to hear the Lord telling you that he wants someone to be healed—now. I think the Lord often offers us a gift of faith, and we decline it because we are afraid to step out and pray with complete confidence.

At the same time, don't immediately lay hands on the sick person and start to pray without asking the Lord what he wants to do. Sometimes the Lord wants you to pray for a spiritual problem or for the person to have a happy death rather than for physical healing.

Realize that you are entering the front line of spiritual warfare when you pray for healing. Take very seriously these words of Paul in Ephesians: "Our battle is not against human forces but against the principalities and powers, the rulers of this world of darkness, the evil spirits in the region above." You will frequently sense a wall, a force, a coldness, a darkness resisting your prayer. Quite often this is the presence of evil that holds the person in bondage. When you detect the work of evil spirits in someone who needs healing, pray with the authority of the Lord Jesus Christ that the spirits be gone.

I will say more about this ministry of deliverance later.

Evil spirits are only one of the many things that can impede our prayer for healing. You probably know some of the other factors if you have ever prayed for a sick family member or close friend. You don't know how to pray. You are sure that the illness in front of you is greater than your faith. You are afraid that the person won't be healed and that you will look like a fool. The result: you either forget about praying for healing or you look for an expert—someone with a "healing ministry"—to do the job.

I know these thoughts. I have had every one of them. But you and I need to pray confidently in spite of them.

The Lord has given special healing ministries to certain individuals, but he also wants every Christian to pray for healing regularly and routinely. We should all heed the words of James: "Pray for one another, that you may find healing."

We should pray in accordance with our relationships. Parents should pray for their sick children. Pastors should pray for their flocks. Confessors should pray for their penitents. Leaders of prayer groups should pray for the people who come for spiritual sustenance. Members of parishes and other groups with a common identity and purpose should pray for each other when they fall ill.

The secular law has a fancy word for this principle: jurisdiction. All of us have jurisdiction—a place in the body of Christ where we have authority and responsibility. Ordinary healing operates as ordinary Christians pray in their sphere of jurisdiction.

Another word for it is love. Our relationships are the channels for healing because that is the way our love flows. God heals us because he loves us. His healing power will flow through us as we pray for those whom we love.

How do we pray? In addition to praying in faith, we should

be alert to three things: praying with perseverance, praying with laying on of hands, and praying with blessed oil.

Blessed oil and laying on of hands have been associated with healing since ancient times. We read in Mark's Gospel that when the twelve went on their first apostolic mission, "they anointed with oil many that were sick and healed them." The priest uses blessed oil in the sacrament of anointing the sick, but it can be used by others for non-sacramental prayer as well. The laying on of hands has become very familiar through the charismatic renewal and healing services. It is a gesture of love and fraternal care that the Lord often uses to impart healing.

The most important thing we can do when we pray for healing is to stick to it. Most people pray for as long as it takes to swallow two aspirin. We will sit in a doctor's waiting room for half a day, but we are reluctant to spend more than a half a minute praying for healing.

Most healing takes time. With a few exceptions, *praying* for healing takes time. It takes time to understand what the problem is, time to see if it is connected with the work of evil spirits or with unrepented sin, time to hear the Lord speak about the situation, time to pray. There are no rules about how long to pray. Sometimes the Lord will lead us to pray in one lengthy session. Sometimes we need to pray two, three, or four times a day for weeks or months—just like the prescription we get from the doctor.

A long-term commitment to prayer for healing often involves pastoral care, particularly when you are dealing with someone's emotional or psychological illness. Very often, a person will not be healed until they change the relationship, the job, the living situation, or the bad habits that caused the problem in the first place. If healed, they will fall back into illness unless these circumstances are changed.

What is received in faith must be maintained in faith. Time and again I have seen people experience a healing and then doubt it. I don't mean that they had a few passing doubts. Most of us have such thoughts. Rather, they gave in to doubt, nurtured it and confessed to themselves or others: "I probably wasn't healed." The faith they had when the healing occurred will disappear and soon they will be sick again.

John Wimber tells a dramatic story to illustrate this point. At a healing session one evening he received a revelation that a woman in a red dress should come forward to receive prayer for a twisted spine. After a few moments, the woman came up. She wore a red dress and was visibly deformed. As Wimber and his team prayed with her, she was healed. She straightened up and walked back to her seat normally while the assembly rejoiced.

A week later the woman came to Wimber's home. Her deformity had reappeared. Her spine was as twisted as it had been before her healing the previous week. Wimber discovered the reason after talking to the woman: her husband had undermined her faith. He had accompanied her to the healing session. He had not wanted her to go up to receive prayer, even though it was obvious that the Lord wanted her healed. When she got back to her seat after being healed, he said, "You know, you made a fool out of yourself up there." The woman thought her husband might be right. Soon her spine was bent again.

The Lord straightened out the woman's spine again when Wimber prayed with her, but this time Wimber was careful to straighten out the husband as well. This healing was maintained only with the right kind of pastoral care.

We must keep healing in perspective. Healing is dramatic. It shows the Lord's love for us in an unmistakable way. But physical and emotional healing are temporary. Lazarus was raised from the dead, but he died again. So too will we all die despite whatever healings we may have experienced.

The most important healing is spiritual, not physical. The most grievous wound we suffer is the breach between ourselves and God. Jesus healed this wound, lifted the intolerable burden of guilt and sin that lies on our shoulders, and took it onto himself. The greatest healing is the healing of the ravages of sin.

The paralytic in Luke 5 was lowered to Jesus through a hole in the roof because the crowds were so great. Once this man was whole. Now he lies there on his bed before his Lord, twisted and helpless. To me this is the physical expression of our spiritual condition. We were created to know, love, and serve God, but we are grievously crippled by our sinful natures and we are unable to do anything about it.

What does Jesus do when this helpless cripple descends into his presence? He says, "Your sins are forgiven you."

This is an astonishing statement. The man was crippled, yet Jesus forgives his sins! His audience was a crowd of scribes and Pharisees who immediately murmured with astonishment at this teacher's audacity at claiming to forgive someone's sins. Jesus immediately detected their hypocrisy. Even though they piously deplored the blasphemy that was implicit in a claim to forgive someone's sins, they thought it was easier for Jesus to say that he had forgiven someone than it was to actually heal his physical paralysis.

So Jesus proceeds to heal the paralytic's physical problem. Why? "To make it clear to you that the Son of Man has authority on earth to forgive sins."

The lesson is clear. Forgiveness of sins is a greater miracle than physical healing. Magicians and sorcerers in Palestine in Jesus' time gave healing to the body. But only God could forgive sins, remove guilt, and free a man's spirit. Only God could transform the inner man that has been blighted by sin.

Physical healing is God's gift to us. We should seek it when we are ill and pray for it whenever we get the chance. Yet we should never seek healing for itself and never forget that healing is a sign of the Lord's desire to repair our sin—the greater wound in our relationship with the Father.

The proper perspective for healing is the perspective of eternity. Full healing of all God's people will not come until the Lord comes again. Until Jesus comes in glory, there will be sickness, death, disappointment, frustration, confusion, and failure—even when we pray.

Smith Wigglesworth, a great nineteenth century evangelist with a powerful healing ministry in the United States and Britain, was a sick man while he ministered healing. He passed hundreds of gallstones during the years that people were healed of grave illnesses when he prayed for them. Wigglesworth is a sign of the church. We do the Lord's work while we are hurting ourselves, and the sinful conditions of our world will always limit the work we can do.

Until the Lord comes again there will be much we do not understand. Once I was present when Kathryn Kuhlman announced that a man was being healed of a chronic back problem that had required him to wear a brace. Soon a man came forward, a bus driver who had driven a church group to the service. He said he was free of pain for the first time in years. He took the brace off. He moved back and forth freely, smiling and laughing. The problem was that he was an unbeliever.

"Do you know that Jesus healed you?" asked Kathryn.

"I don't know who healed me," the man said.

"Well, you heard us praying to Jesus. You heard me say that Jesus healed you. Who do you think healed you?"

"I dunno. I just know I'm healed."

"*Why* do you think you were healed?"

"I don't know."

The man steadfastly refused to entertain the idea that Jesus healed him because he loved him, and that the Lord had a greater healing in mind if he would simply make a confession of faith. He resisted the good news perversely.

A woman sitting next to me listened to all this for a while and then began pounding the pew in anger.

"That's not fair," she raged. "I've been coming here every week for three years and I haven't been healed, but that man was healed and he doesn't even believe."

I sympathized with the woman even as I prayed that her anger wouldn't cause her to curse God. We really don't know very much. We know that anything *can* be healed, but not everything *will* be healed. We know that the experience of enduring illness can build character. We know that suffering has a redemptive quality to it. We don't know why some people are healed and some are not, but we do know that all will be made whole when we are with the Lord. It is better to die young and spend eternity with the Lord than it is to live a full and healthy life on earth and lose eternal life. It is better to struggle for decades with mental illness and go to heaven than it is to be emotionally whole and end up in hell.

My friend Fr. Ed McDonough once put the whole thing in perspective at a huge healing service that he was conducting in a tent on the campus of the University of Steubenville. Thousands of people were present; most of them were hoping to be healed that evening, drawn by the news that thousands of people have experienced healing through Fr. McDonough's ministry. That evening, Fr. McDonough looked out at the crowd and said an astonishing thing.

"The greatest healing of all would be if this tent got struck by lightning and we all died," he said. "Then we would all be in glory with the Lord. That is the place where we want to be and that is the place where we would be healed completely."

And yet, God is doing an astounding work in the world today through healing. The outpouring of healing graces today seems to be virtually unprecedented in the history of the church. When I was in the seminary I was inspired by accounts of miraculous events in the lives of the saints. I used to hope that I would someday just be present when something miraculous happened.

What I have seen has been staggering. I have stood next to a blind woman whose sight was suddenly restored. I have been within a few feet of deaf people who were suddenly able to hear again. I have watched cripples throw away their crutches and canes and walk. I have seen very sick people get out of their hospital beds and go home. These things are happening in every nation, on every continent, and in every Christian church. Literally millions of people have personal firsthand knowledge of God's healing love.

One day it occurred to me that this vast outpouring of healing graces had a meaning beyond itself. I asked the Lord what it meant. He led me to a passage in Matthew 11 which recounted the story of some other men who asked the Lord what something meant.

They were disciples of John the Baptist. They came to Jesus with a question: "Are you he who is to come, or shall we look for another?" Jesus answered them: "Go and tell John what you hear and see: the blind receive their sight and the lame walk, lepers are cleansed and the deaf hear, and the dead are raised up, and the poor have good news preached to them."

Of these six signs, five involve physical healing.

When Jesus was asked to identify himself, he pointed to his healing work. Healing, in short, is a way the Lord announces his presence among his people. Our response should be the same as that of John's disciples: we have found him!

I believe that the healing we see all over the world signifies a new urgency in the Lord's work in the world. This is a time of visitation. He is announcing his presence unmistakably. Those who see it will be saved; those who avert their eyes to the Savior's work will be lost.

On Palm Sunday, Jesus came into Jerusalem amid shouts of praise. The people had seen his works—his miracle of raising Lazarus from the dead—and they proclaimed him as Messiah. When the Pharisees told him to quiet his followers, Jesus turned on them sharply. "If these were silent," he said, "the very stones would cry out."

But most of the city *was* silent. The people refused to see Jesus in the miraculous healings that they all knew about. Jesus wept over Jerusalem and prophesied the judgment that came on it in 70 A.D.: "the time shall come upon you, when your enemies will cast up a bank about you ... and dash you to the ground, you and your children within you, and they will not leave one stone upon another in you; because you did not know the time of your visitation."

We are in a similar time of visitation. It is following the same course as the visitation Luke describes. It starts with signs, wonders, healings, and resurrections—the miracles we have been seeing all over the world. These point to Jesus. Their purpose is to show him as the Lord and Messiah, the Savior and Master to whom all lives should be submitted. The next step is to purify God's house. Just as Jesus' first action upon entering Jerusalem was to drive the traders out of the temple, our task is to renew the church and equip it to do his work. The outcome of this visitation is to create a people wholly submitted to the Lord, a people of holiness who can reign with him in glory forever.

But this work involves struggle. This is the next step in a renewed life with the Lord—the fact that we are in the middle of a spiritual battle between armies that take no prisoners.

TWELVE

There's a War Going On

FOR AS LONG AS I CAN REMEMBER, I worked hard to be known as a nice guy. I tried to smooth over disagreements among my friends. I settled disputes in the committee meetings where I spent so much of my time. I cultivated the habit of always looking at the bright side of things. And I really believed that the bright side was the right side. I didn't like gloomy talk. I didn't think there was any problem that men and women of sincerity and goodwill couldn't solve.

I liked it when people smiled as I walked into a room.

In this I was a typical American. Europeans can be gloomy. Americans tend to be optimistic, upbeat, and positive. The sky's the limit. Things are always getting better. No obstacle is so great that it cannot be overcome.

My cheerful American spirit responded warmly to the upbeat atmosphere of the Catholic church in the years following Vatican Council II. The Council reached out to Protestants and non-Christians—people whom the Catholic church had hardly been friendly with over the centuries—and proclaimed the church's openness to ideas and institutions that advanced human welfare. The Council's goal was to better equip the church for evangelism in modern conditions, but this evangelical mission somehow got lost in most of the talk about "the spirit of Vatican II." The atmosphere in church circles at the time was one of uncritical affirmation of just about every person, institution, and movement that we encountered. People talked about love and peace as if we could attain them merely by talking about them. We Catholics thought that everyone should be our friend. I assimilated these sentimental notions, as did many other Catholics.

I even thought seriously about pacifism in the early 1970s. I thought I understood why so many Christian pacifists drew inspiration from St. Francis of Assisi, the great lover of man, beast, and all of nature. I later realized that this is a sentimental misinterpretation of the Franciscan ideal. Francis actually saw himself as a warrior for the Lord Jesus, and he did fierce battle with evil throughout his life. Nevertheless, I began to think that non-violence could overcome violence, that literally turning the other cheek when confronted by wrongdoing was the Lord's response to evil.

I hadn't yet experienced the unmistakable signs of evil spirits in others, and my theoretical knowledge of their existence didn't make an impact on me.

Paul explained the basic facts of spiritual warfare in a well-known passage. "We are not contending against flesh and blood," he wrote in Ephesians, "but against the principalities, against the powers, against the world rulers of this present darkness, against the spiritual hosts of wickedness in the heavenly places."

Peter says that our "adversary the devil prowls around like a roaring lion seeking someone to devour."

First John says that "the reason the Son of God appeared was to destroy the works of the devil."

Tertullian, one of the early fathers of the church, said this about evil spirits: "Their business is to corrupt mankind; thus, the spirit of evil was from the very beginning bent upon man's destruction. The demons, therefore, inflict upon men's bodies diseases and other bitter misfortunes, and upon the soul sudden and extraordinary outbursts of violence."

Around the time when I was flirting with pacifism, Pope Paul VI asked a general audience "What are the greatest needs of the church today?" and gave an answer that must have startled many of his listeners: "defense from that evil which is called the Devil." He described the Devil as "the cunning enchanter who finds his way into us by way of the senses, the imagination, the lust, utopian logic, or disorderly social contacts in the give-and-take of life."

Satan knows us only too well. He perverts our good human qualities. He takes our sexual drive and directs it toward fornication and adultery. He takes our aggressiveness and desire to succeed and tempts us to cheat and lie and crush our competitors. He takes our emotions, which God gave us for our good, and perverts them into weaknesses that will lead us to sin.

It took a brush with death at the hands of a woman under bondage to remind me that the Christian life is a life of struggle. This woman, in the midst of prayer for deliverance, came at me with a kitchen knife.

We are in a war. Satan is trying to knock us out of the battle. He would like to kill us. The pacifist response to Satan would have been literally fatal when this woman attacked me. It would be spiritually fatal to look at my work for the Lord in these terms. Non-violence doesn't affect the kingdom of evil. It simply allows evil to have its way.

The Christian life is serious business. It's a war.

The truth about the struggle between good and evil is found in Scripture. After my close encounter with death, I did a Scripture study about Satan and evil. What I discovered ran contrary to the resurgence of love and peace and friendliness that cascaded through the Catholic church in the early 1970s.

The good news is a message of salvation. Salvation from what? Not from poverty, or narrow-mindedness, or oppressive authority, or outmoded traditions. But salvation from sin. "You will die in your sins unless you believe that I am he," Jesus said (Jn 8:24). Sin is not simply one of the many things in our human make-up, something like our relationships, our work, our race, or our nationality. It is literally the governing element of our being. Sin holds us in slavery. It rules us.

The slavemaster is a person, or persons. Before we were Christians, Paul writes, "we were slaves to the elemental spirits of the universe" (Gal 4:3). Elsewhere Scripture calls him the "ruler of this world" (Jn 12:31). This is Satan, the tempter, the deceiver, the destroyer. He is so bold that he even tempted Jesus himself. The Lord refused Satan's offer of all the kingdoms of the world, but he didn't dispute the fact that the kingdoms of the world were Satan's to give.

Jesus overthrew Satan's rule. He personally subdued the tempter in the struggle in the desert. He broke Satan's hold on individuals whenever he had the opportunity. On the cross, he broke Satan's hold on mankind for all time and established the Kingdom of God that will last forever.

The gospel proclaims this Kingdom and invites all men and women to be freed from Satan's rule. We enter the Kingdom by being joined to Christ by faith. This frees us from our bondage to sin. "The slave does not continue in the house for ever," John writes. "The son continues for ever. So if the Son makes you free, you will be free indeed."

Even though we are free, the battle still rages between two kingdoms. It is like a war that continues after the decisive battle has already been fought. The Lord invites every man and woman to receive love, forgiveness, and abundant life in God's Kingdom. Satan struggles to keep us out of God's Kingdom and in bondage to him. The Lord wants everyone to join God's family and enjoy eternal life. Satan wants to isolate us and ultimately cast us into eternal death in hell. The Lord wants to use his people to spread the good news throughout the earth. Satan will do anything to make us timid, troubled, and ineffective servants of our Master.

There is no basis for peaceful coexistence between God's Kingdom and Satan's. There can be only opposition and bitter struggle. We are born in the midst of this war. We are both the soldiers in the armies and the battleground upon which the war takes place. Our eternal destiny is what the war is all about.

We cannot be indifferent to the fact that there's a war going on. The war doesn't stop because *you* don't believe in it. You can't opt out of the battle because warfare doesn't appeal to you. The war is a fact, a dangerous fact that you ignore to your own peril.

Many Christians, however, do ignore the war. I remember discussing my Scripture study about Satan and evil with a pacifist priest friend. I told him about my conviction that Satan is a real, personal enemy, that we are all involved in a spiritual war, that I knew that evil spirits are at work in all of us. My friend was worried about me.

"Mike," he said, "the devil was fine for the Middle Ages when people were superstitious and the priests needed an image to keep them in line. But we're grown-up adults now. We don't need the devil any more."

"We don't need him but we've got him," I replied. "What about Scripture? Who tempted Jesus in the desert? What were those spirits that Jesus cast out of people?"

"Symbols. Those are symbols. The temptation in the desert means that Jesus overcame the tendency within himself to do wrong. Then he taught other people to do the same thing. He healed some of those people of psychological problems. The writers of Scripture expressed this in terms of Satan and evil spirits because that's the way people in the first century understood those things. But they certainly weren't real evil spirits."

I thought about the woman with the kitchen knife. I recalled another woman who had recently come to me for deliverance prayer. I will call her Gail. She was a married woman from out of town who was obviously oppressed by evil spirits. Her pastors had not been able to help her.

I led a group of five people who prayed with Gail. Just as the prayer started, a frightening change came over her. A livid, fiery look came on her face; her eyes burned like coals; her tongue darted in and out of her mouth like the tongue of a snake who was attacking its prey. It was a terrifying revelation of Satan.

"I'm going to kill you," the spirit growled in a man's voice.

"No, you're not," I growled back. "I'm going to get rid of you."

We snarled at each other for many minutes, me ordering the spirit out, the spirit cursing, objecting, struggling with us to escape its fate. A woman who was present said later that the abuse was so violent that she thought she was in hell. Finally he left at my shouted, authoritative command to depart in the name of the Lord Jesus Christ. Gail experienced immediate relief and has remained free of oppression from evil spirits ever since.

Symbols? I recalled the ninety-pound coed at the College of Steubenville who knocked me to the ground with superhuman strength in the middle of prayer for deliverance. It took all my strength to physically restrain her so that I could force the evil spirits that oppressed her to obey my command to leave.

No, evil spirits are not symbols. They are real enemies.

Nothing is too small or too large, too human or too spiritual to escape Satan's attention. From the daily events of our personal lives to the complex workings of huge governments and organizations, Satan and his evil spirits find ways to infect the world and the church.

I have seen the work of evil spirits in the lives of individuals so often that I am convinced that the reason why so many Christians do not live in the full freedom of the sons and daughters of God is that many areas of their lives are in bondage to Satan. Sins, bad habits, physical illness, emotional wounds, psychological problems, "bad luck," broken relationships, fears, compulsions, and problems in relating to God are just some of the ways that Satan may wage war against us.

Fortunately, in deliverance prayer we have the tool we need to deal with the work of Satan.

Every Christian should regularly use the deliverance weapon against Satan. I recommend *Deliverance from Evil Spirits,* a book I wrote with Randy Cirner, for a complete discussion of the scriptural and theological background of deliverance and the pastoral context in which it should take place. Even though some aspects of deliverance can get fairly involved, the essence of deliverance is simple. When you detect the presence of an evil spirit in yourself or others, you order it to leave.

Larry is a good example. Larry was a successful businessman who came to me complaining of restlessness and anxiety. Larry met with me and another man who works with me in the Christian community we are part of in Steubenville. As we talked, Larry came across as a highly ambitious man who was constantly frustrated because he could never achieve the goals or satisfy the standards he set for himself. Anger boiled inside him. There was also something else, a sense of hopelessness, of being trapped.

I could see no good reason for the hopelessness; it didn't fit with the rest of Larry's personality. To me that was a sign of the presence of an evil spirit. Pockets of irrational emotion or unexplainable behavior are often signals that something is under the control of a spirit.

We prayed. Sure enough, the Lord gave me a strong sense that Larry was being afflicted by a spirit of despair. Spirits of pessimism, self-pity, and resentment were connected to it. The three of us simply commanded the spirits to depart. I said something like this: "By the power of Jesus Christ who is our Lord and whom we serve, and with the authority of Christ, I command you, spirit of despair, to leave Larry this very moment. I break your hold on him. I cast you out."

We ministered to Larry in many other ways. We prayed for healing of the memories of two painful events in his life. We prayed for the gift of hope. He repented of sins against hope and of an ambition that often superseded God's plan for his life. We worked out a plan of prayer and Scripture study and fellowship with other men that would protect him from falling prey to sin and Satan again.

But the simple deliverance from those spirits was a breakthrough for Larry. He was suddenly free in areas that had been under bondage. By ordering the spirits to depart, he was free to be righteous and holy.

I have seen the same thing happen hundreds of times. People who couldn't stop eating, or masturbating, or drinking, or cursing were able to stop when the spirit that was controlling this behavior was identified and expelled. I have seen men and women whose personalities were dominated by anger and rebellion change when they were delivered of evil spirits. Behavior and disorderly emotions that wouldn't change through counseling or prayer or repentance would change quickly because someone identified a spirit and ordered him out in the name of Jesus Christ.

The same irrational behavior can characterize groups and whole institutions. After decades of work in dozens of different Christian organizations, I have become convinced that many programs fail or are less effective than they should be because they are diabolically harassed. I am sure that the same thing is true of secular organizations. Institutions, like individuals, can come under evil oppression that must be squarely faced and dealt with.

If Satan cannot lure us away from the Kingdom of God, he is content to render us ineffective. He succeeds if he can deflect us from God's plan for us, even if we do some good for some people. His tactic is fear. Our only real fear is fear of separation from the Lord—hardly an imminent fear if we are faithful to his word. But Satan will try to incapacitate us with other fears—fear for our economic security, fear of change, fear of failing, fear of looking foolish, even fear of evil spirits. Sadly, many individuals and institutions in the church are ineffective precisely because they are afraid to act.

The other danger is failure to see that there's a war going on.

We have no choice about the war. Nobody asked us whether we want to fight. We can't get out of it. Since we are going to spend eternity in heaven with the other soldiers, the most important perspective on our lives will be what we did in the war.

We might talk about the battle—about raising our children in the midst of a hostile culture, about overcoming temptation and repenting of sin and carrying on day after day, about boredom and taking losses and fighting the temptation to give up, about using our strengths and compensating for our weaknesses, about expelling evil spirits from our lives and from others we are close to, about befriending the friendless and serving the needy and preaching the gospel, about acting in the power of the Holy Spirit instead of our own power, about doing the Lord's will instead of our own, about how hard it was to make and keep commitments, about how hard it was to live a life serving others, and about how glorious is our reward.

In the months after I was baptized in the Spirit, I used to be a little irritated by older priests who cautioned me about not getting caught up in "spiritual experience" or "enthusiasm." I was *very* enthusiastic. Praying in tongues was wonderful. I was amazed and delighted to hear the Lord speak to me and to read the Bible like it was a personal letter from the Father to me. Perhaps the priests who held back a little were not as open to spiritual experience as they should have been, but I think at least some of them were right. They were telling me that the charismatic experience is not an end in itself but is given for a reason—to equip us for battle.

There's a certain progression in all this. We are baptized in the Holy Spirit and receive power. We restore our relationship with the Lord by repentance. We discover the mighty healing work in the Kingdom. Then we learn that we are in a war.

The next step is to take our place in this war.

THIRTEEN

A Mission at Steubenville

Pentecost Sunday, 1974, was a day for rejoicing and thanksgiving. A warm sun had burned the mist off the Appalachian hills by late morning and the day turned crystal clear. Every detail of the landscape leapt out at me as I walked away from the seminary after Mass. It was a day when creation spoke of its creator. The world looked more real than real. The outlines of trees and leaves were etched permanently against the deep blue sky.

I would have relished being a contemplative monk, I thought as I walked through the splendid hills. I had chosen— no, been led to—one of the most active branches of the mighty Franciscan tree. I liked running a seminary, writing books, and pastoring people until I couldn't keep my eyes open any more. But I could have walked down the Carnaldolese or Carthusian path as well. These are monks who live in solitude. I yearned for solitude. Give me time for prayer, hours of time, day after day to praise God and hear his voice. Give me a hut in a countryside like this.

I began to thank God as I walked. Thank you, Lord, for the firm and close relationships you have given me with brothers and sisters in the prayer group and in the seminary. Thank you for baptizing me in your Holy Spirit. Thank you for the gifts you have given me that have transformed my priestly ministry. Thank you for renewing my mind. I went on to thank him for blessing a number of people I knew: a seminarian delivered from depression, a ruined marriage healed, a child's recovery from a serious injury, a job for a man who had been out of work, a nun's new confidence in her work.

Then I started to thank the Lord for directing me down *this* path in my life and not others. This is something I often do when my work isn't going well and I am troubled or exhausted. We can revive our spirits by reminding ourselves that we are all richly blessed by God even when the circumstances of our lives seem bleak or even hopeless. Praying this way was easy on this Pentecost because I had rarely felt so exuberant.

I could be a politician or a diplomat or a well-to-do lawyer on Wall Street right now. Thank you, Lord, for not letting me do any of those things or take any of the other paths I could have taken. Thank you for calling me to the priesthood and for the grace to respond to that call. Thank you for guiding me to the Third Order Regular Franciscans. Thank you for not letting me be a missionary, or an academic theologian, or canon lawyer, my choices for priestly work. Thank you for calling me to be rector of St. Francis Seminary.

I could see how the seminary was the right place for me. My education and past experience had all led up to it. It was a solid base for the other work the Lord was leading me into through the charismatic renewal.

I was standing in an opening in the woods, a place called Barkovich Park, named after one of the seminary cooks. I was looking at the sky, caught up in the immensity of God.

The thought of Steubenville crossed my mind. Steubenville. The smoky, grimy, industrial city where I had spent several years as a dean. What a contrast. I'm glad I'm not in Steubenville. I decided to thank the Lord for something that had been troubling me in the past months.

Thank you, Lord, that I don't have to respond to the overtures my provincial has been making to let my name be considered for the presidency of the College of Steubenville. Thank you that I don't have to go back there and listen to professors argue in interminable faculty meetings about required courses. Thank you that I can be based in a seminary, where there is real faith, and not in a college, where there's hardly any faith to speak of any more. Thank you that I don't have to wheel and deal to get key administrators and faculty members to agree to my budget. Thank you that I don't have to listen to students complain about cafeteria food and dormatory curfews.

Then the Lord spoke, quietly but clearly.

"What if I want you to be president of the College of Steubenville?"

It was like the moment on Longfellow's property when the Lord asked me if I would give him my whole life. I was paralyzed. A new vista was opening up. The ground was shaking beneath my feet. I thought for a few moments, and then made a response like the one I made at Harvard. I equivocated.

"Okay Lord. If you want me to be president of Steubenville, I'll do it. But I'm pretty sure you don't want it."

But it soon became obvious to me that my response was inadequate. I had to pursue this possible direction before I knew whether the Lord wanted it. The Lord calls each of us to do a job in his Kingdom but he never *insists* that we do what he wishes. He issues invitations. He prods. He puts the idea in our minds, sometimes at the edges of our minds, and measures our response. We need to respond. Hearing the Lord and following him usually involves a tedious process of thinking things through and checking things out. I honestly did not know whether the Lord wanted me to be president of the College of Steubenville. I knew that *I* didn't want to do it. When the Lord spoke in the hills, he was letting me know, gently enough, that my preferences weren't necessarily his.

So I checked out my reluctance to be a college president.

I discussed the idea with three other priests, Dan, Sam, and Augustine, whom I relied on for spiritual and personal support. The four of us had made a commitment to share our lives in a seriously committed way. We protected each other from the spiritual attacks and personal confusions that are so common in religious life. Our commitment and our unity made us stronger and more confident in our work. Our spiritual lives deepened as we prayed together. And we consistently came up with better decisions as a group than we could have made individually.

That seminary covenant group was my first real taste of Christian community. I loved it. I am now part of a much larger Christian community in Steubenville called the Servants of Christ the King. Several hundred married couples, single people, and priests have made covenant commitments similar to the ones we four priests made in Loretto. This kind of covenant commitment turned out to be a key to renewing and rebuilding the College of Steubenville.

My brother priests were skeptical about the presidency question. They did, however, think I should meet with the search committee to give it some ideas about what a Christian college should be like.

The provincial agreed with that approach. He asked me to meet with the search committee if only to let them talk to someone he thought was qualified for the job. I didn't need to actually consider taking the position.

As I talked over the idea, my own thinking crystallized. I was very uncomfortable with the idea of my major work being college administration, even if it was a Catholic college with public Christian ideals.

It was sure to be a very difficult job. The early 1970s were years of crisis for most colleges and universities in the United States. The pool of college-age young people was shrinking. Colleges which had expanded rapidly as the post-war baby boom generation came to college age began to compete for students as this generation graduated.

Inflation pushed up the cost of a college education while recession reduced the ability of many families to pay for it. No longer did a college degree automatically lead to a good job.

Young people and their parents looked at a college program very carefully and rejected the weaker schools.

Only the strongest schools could flourish in such an environment. One heard dire predictions that hundreds of private liberal arts colleges would be forced to close down, victims of fiscal pressure, a shrinking pool of potential students, and the growing emphasis on vocationally-oriented education.

The College of Steubenville was precisely the kind of school that faced a very rocky road in these hard times. It was small, poorly endowed, relatively new, and little known. The college had begun in 1946 as a commuter school primarily serving ex-servicemen who had GI Bill money to spend on a college education. For years classes were held in rooms all over downtown Steubenville. Sometimes the college's finances were so shaky in those early years that students would call on Monday morning to see if the school was still open.

In the early 1960s a wealthy benefactor donated land and the college moved to its current campus on a hill overlooking the Ohio River. Dormatories were built and residential students enrolled. Nevertheless, the long-term health of the college was hardly assured. The new president would likely be leading the college in a struggle for survival, not an era of exciting growth.

One pressure on the president would surely be to blur the college's Christian character and become more like a secular school. Almost all the Catholic colleges and universities I knew about were abandoning or soft-pedaling their Christian character. They wanted to succeed professionally, and many administrators and faculty thought this meant embracing the secular dogma that religious norms had no intellectual standing in an institution devoted to objective truth. Student life at Steubenville and the other Catholic colleges I knew about was increasingly permissive, individualistic, hedonistic, and riddled with drugs, alcohol, and sex.

I did not relish the idea of running a college, any college. Colleges are collections of interest groups that are suspicious of each other and protective of their status and prerogatives. A college in crisis—a school like Steubenville—needed strong leadership from a president with abundant executive authority. But most college presidents have very little real authority. The most successful college presidents were those with the patience to listen sympathetically to everyone's ideas and complaints and the diplomatic skills to mediate disputes among people who don't want to listen to each other.

Was this what I wanted to do?

I wanted to be where I saw the Holy Spirit moving. I frankly did not see him working on the Catholic campuses of the United States. He was moving in the charismatic renewal, in Christian communities like the Word of God in Ann Arbor, in healing ministries, in grass roots ecumenical movements, in parts of evangelical Protestantism, in a few Catholic outreaches to the poor that I admired, in the scattered but growing movement to renew Catholic worship, prayer, and Scripture study. The golden age of Catholic higher education had passed. I wanted to be on the crest of the wave, not the backwash.

In short, I was genuinely puzzled about why the Lord might want me to be a president of a Catholic college.

As I was mulling over this problem, I went to the International Conference on the Catholic Charismatic Renewal at Notre Dame. I love the fellowship at these conferences, and at each a speaker has said something that altered my life. At that conference, a speaker said something about the Steubenville problem.

The speaker was Dr. Robert Frost, a Protestant Pentecostal leader who had left a scientific career for full-time Christian ministry. Frost told us how the Lord had called him to ever-deeper commitments and greater responsibilities. He had responded to these calls, Frost said, but he had always held something back. I listened carefully. This story sounded familiar.

One day Frost realized why he had never given his life fully to the Lord. The reason sounded ludicrous at first, but it was very real. He was afraid that if he did whatever the Lord wanted, the Lord would send him to Africa, where he would be surrounded by pygmies with spears. It was a real fear. Frost didn't want to be murdered in Africa.

Frost eventually overcame the fear and submitted his life to the Lord completely. When he did, the fear left. Then Frost said something that had a mighty impact on me.

He said: "I found out that the Lord never calls you to Africa without first putting Africa in your heart."

At that moment, Steubenville came into my heart. That dirty milltown. That college facing a host of problems that threatened its survival. I wanted to go there. It was the only place I wanted to go. I could see myself being a priest in Steubenville, doing all kinds of work that the Lord wanted done, ministering his love and mercy to students, faculty, administrators, townspeople, and being ministered to by them. The problems and questions were still there, but now I didn't care. If the Lord wanted me to go to Steubenville, I would go eagerly. When I returned to the seminary, I told the provincial that I would let the search committee talk to me.

As the interview approached, I realized that I would probably be staying at St. Francis Seminary after all. The committee wouldn't want me when they got to know me. My ideas about what the college should be called for radical changes, and I would take the job only if I could implement them. I doubted that the members of the search committee shared my vision, and I could not imagine that the board of trustees would give me the authority I needed to make this vision a reality. Bob Frost never had to live in Africa. As I went to meet the search committee, I was fairly sure I would never have to go back to Steubenville.

I met with the search committee one warm June morning in Steubenville. The committee members, representing faculty, students, administration, and the board of trustees, interviewed two candidates before me and one afterward. They looked tired and a bit anxious. I later learned why. The other candidates had been recommending that the trustees hire a president who could shut the College of Steubenville down or persuade the state of Ohio to take it over.

I told the committee something very different. The school was in trouble, I said, because academic concerns and money worries were taking everyone's attention. Spiritual matters had to take priority. Not only did we need to restore the college's Franciscan Catholic identity in all its historic splendor, but a vibrant, dynamic Christian faith had to dominate and shape the environment. This would not happen, I said, unless academic and financial concerns were subordinate to spiritual health.

To accomplish this, I said I would lead an effort to return the college to the spirit of the first Franciscans. Francis and his first followers were charismatic, so I would cultivate a strong charismatic presence on the campus. Because the search committee included Protestant, Jewish, and possibly agnostic members, I described the charismatic renewal in some detail. I told them that the charismatic renewal embodied the kind of dynamic faith that I thought should shape the college life, a faith marked by free praise of the Lord, spiritual gifts, commitments to one another's welfare, and a life of prayer. The charismatic renewal would be the base for a renewal in theological studies.

The vision was to return the college to its Franciscan roots. It would prosper by becoming a place where the gospel was freely and openly proclaimed, where relationships were conducted according to the patterns of Christian community, where the ideal of life was surrender to the Lord Jesus and desire to serve him.

My program for Steubenville was novel to say the least. Spiritual matters rarely take priority over academic and financial concerns in a college. Although colleges like to portray themselves as communities of scholars devoted to academic excellence, the reality is usually very different. Most schools are dominated by curriculum decisions and financial pressures. I was proposing to give top priority to spiritual renewal at a time when money was tight and most students and parents were looking for academic quality above all else.

My enthusiasm for the charismatic renewal must have sounded odd too. How could a controversial spiritual renewal movement featuring glossolalia, healing, and other spiritual gifts ignite a renewal of Franciscan Catholic spirituality in what was increasingly known as a party school?

Finally, I chose to deliver this message to the search committee in prophetic terms. I spoke about what God wanted in a college that was both Catholic and Franciscan. As I was talking, it occurred to me that some members of the search committee might have thought that they were interviewing someone too pious to be realistic.

If they did, they kept that opinion to themselves. That evening, the provincial told me that the search committee had decided to recommend only one candidate to the board of trustees—me. The vote was nearly unanimous. Fr. Columba told me to think about it.

Two weeks later Fr. Columba took me out to dinner, an extraordinary gesture from a no-nonsense man who thought dinners and parties were excuses to waste time. After a few pleasantries he announced his business.

"The board of trustees wants you," he said. "There are no other candidates. I'm here to get your consent."

I was torn. I thought I had heard the Lord about being president of Steubenville, yet I had made commitments to people at the seminary that I did not think I could voluntarily break. I still had many reservations about being a college president. Why did the Lord want me to do this?

We discussed these questions. Fr. Columba said he could replace me at the seminary. He too thought I was the only one for the college.

"What about the promises I made to people at the seminary?" I asked. "I've started programs. People have come there to be with me."

"We'll get the job done somehow," he said.

"But I don't feel free to decide on my own to leave."

"Let me do it for you. I'll put you under obedience and order you to leave."

That turned out to be the solution. In the final analysis, I was a man under obedience to earthly superiors as well as to God. I didn't make my own decisions. Neither did I carry my burdens or resolve dilemmas like the one I was facing on my own. How appropriate it was for a Franciscan to take on major new responsibilities as a man under obedience.

One more task had to be overcome. I wanted to speak to the board of trustees directly to let them know what was coming and get the authorization to make the changes I wanted to make. Maybe they were hiring me because I was the only candidate for president who didn't want to shut the college down. Maybe they thought the situation was so desperate that they decided to throw the dice and hire a president who they thought could save the college through prayer and spiritual gifts. But I wanted them to hear it from me.

I met the board and told it the same things I had told the search committee. They agreed to give me authority to do everything I outlined—an extraordinary amount of power for a college president to have.

I ended my address with an expression of confidence: "If we do all this and still the college fails and I am the last president of the College of Steubenville, it won't bother me at all as long as we did the right things."

In July, 1969, I had left Steubenville to take up a job I knew I couldn't do—supervise the formation of seminarians at St. Francis Seminary. I had been worried and anxious.

Five years later I packed a car again and returned to Steubenville to be president of the college—a job I was unqualified for. Yet I was confident and content.

Why the difference? I had been baptized in the Spirit. I knew the personal love of the Lord and I experienced his loving care. My relationship with him was right because I had repented. I knew the Lord as a healer and mender, and I understood that the work he was having me do was my mission in a war. Now I had received my particular orders in this battle.

Was the job at Steubenville impossible? That meant it was up to the Lord. I had to rely on the Lord for everything. So did the college. We couldn't be in a better spot than that.

I was also filled with a sense of mission, both for myself and for the college. The College of Steubenville was going to survive and become something unique. The Lord had a particular place for that school in his plan for the years immediately ahead. I thought the same thing for myself. The Lord had been preparing me for years to do one thing. Here it was. He was doing a lot in the world, much more than I even knew about. Here was my little part in it.

I think the same thing is true for all of us. Each of us has work to do in the Kingdom of God, a task that is suited for us and which is part of the great scope of the Lord's work on the earth today. It may take us a while to find this place of service. It may well turn out to be something you never dreamed you would be doing. But when you find this ministry, you will be comfortable. My good friend Fr. John Bertolucci is a preacher. Many things wear him out, but preaching never does. I know scholars who are most comfortable when studying, men and women with healing ministries who never tire out while praying for healing for hours, teachers who are never more comfortable than when they are teaching.

I felt very comfortable heading west to be president of the College of Steubenville.

FOURTEEN

Rebuild My Church

THE WEEK BEFORE I was scheduled to start work as president of the college, I went to Assisi on a pilgrimage of renewal. I wanted to renew the Franciscan fire in my own heart. I wanted a better understanding of the Franciscan vision of renewal I hoped to bring to the college. I wanted guidance if the Saint and his Lord would give it to me. I had confidently told the college trustees that I would do the right things at Steubenville no matter what the consequences. But I wasn't sure what the right things were. So much needed to be done. I had no clear idea of my priorities.

I traveled light with a friend of mine, Bill Callaghan. His wife Lee, under a sense of God's call, had saved money so that I could someday travel to Assisi. We took only carry on luggage on the overseas flight. Only hours after leaving New York I was praying before the San Damiano Cross in the Santa Chiara Church in Assisi, the cross from the ruined church where Francis found refuge shortly after his conversion.

As I prayed, I reflected on these early years of the Franciscans. The Lord spoke to Francis as he prayed in the rubble of San Damiano Church. "Rebuild my house, which lies before you in ruins," he said. Literalist that he was, Francis instantly began to rebuild San Damiano, and he proceeded to repair three other churches in the area. The first Franciscans were men who joined Francis in this repair work.

Later Francis realized that the church the Lord intended him to rebuild was the universal church and that the stones he was to use in the rebuilding were the people God was sending him—first the men, then Clare and her holy women, then the lay people who became the third order. The little poor man walked to Rome to tell the pope about his vision, a journey that more worldly-wise priests told him was foolish. The pope will never see you, they said. But the night before Francis arrived, the pope had a dream. The church was falling down but this little man was holding it up. The next day he recognized Francis as the little man in his dream, and he blessed his plan for a ministry of renewal through poverty, simplicity, brotherhood, repentance, and reconciliation.

Here was the vision for the College of Steubenville: "Rebuild my church." The mission of the college would be to participate in the Lord's ministry of renewal in the Catholic church. Our goal would be faithfulness to God's plan, not success in influence, growth, wealth, or other worldly criteria. The stones for rebuilding would be people: the students at the college and men and women who shared the vision of renewal through a living faith and lives of simplicity and holiness.

Today a frieze showing St. Francis carrying a stone for rebuilding San Damiano decorates the university administration building. I am inspired every time I look at it. It captures the essence of what the university should be.

I heard another word as I walked the same hills where St. Francis walked and dreamed. It was, "build an environment of faith."

Those responsible for church institutions often use words like these—faith environment, community of faith, people of faith. Often these words lack much spiritual content. They are just labels attached to very ordinary and even very worldly institutions and groups of people.

If Steubenville was to be a faith environment, what did that mean?

It seemed to me that a genuine faith environment would

support certain kinds of behavior. Is it easier in this place to grow in your Christian faith or to lose it? Does the atmosphere—the talk, the entertainment, the people—make it easier to be moral and honest and sexually chaste, or does it foster immorality and dishonesty? Is this the kind of place where you could comfortably say that you are a serious Christian, or is that something you would rather keep to yourself? What happens to people over time? After a few years, are people more committed, more mature, more creative, or are they more cynical and disillusioned than when they came?

I had to admit that the College of Steubenville—along with most other Catholic colleges as well as many parishes, religious houses, high schools, social action programs and the rest—would not be judged as faith environments according to these criteria.

I also thought that a faith environment would foster a vital, faith-filled spiritual atmosphere. Were people learning to rely on the Lord, or did they operate according to purely human wisdom and capacity? When the work didn't go well, did people turn to the Lord for consolation and direction, or did they complain and give up? Were people willing to take risks to do what the Lord wanted of them? Were the gifts of the Spirit operating? Were people growing in holiness?

I didn't think the college was a faith environment according to these criteria either.

These questions gave me some clues about what a faith environment should be. The word "environment" was important. The problem wasn't the academic program or the student chaplaincy or the administration or any other part of the college. The whole atmosphere of the place wasn't right. The "system" was wrong. What was needed was a series of changes over time that would eventually alter the system and transform the whole atmosphere of the college. This would be a step-by-step process over time, but it would be guided by a clear understanding of the eventual goal—a spiritual transformation.

As I prayerfully surveyed the complex life of the college, it became clear to me that the first priority was changing student life. Students were the most volatile part of the college community. Individual young people could change rapidly. Next year, a third of the student body would be different. In four years, all the students would be new. Students could change more readily than faculty, who were older and tenured, or administrators, who for the most part affected the life of the college indirectly.

And what's a college for if not for the well-being of its students? Big mega-universities emphasized research and graduate study and influencing public policy. A small college like Steubenville existed to educate young people who were just becoming adults. Everything that happened on the campus had to contribute to their spiritual, intellectual, and social maturity.

I spent my first three months on campus getting to know students. I went to every party I could find. I played tennis, touch football, volleyball, and basketball with them. I ate in the cafeteria with students. I kept an open door and saw students individually or in groups whenever they dropped by.

Student life was appalling.

Alcohol and drugs were the currency of college social life. Alcohol flowed freely at every party, much too freely. Many of the students routinely got drunk on Saturday night and slept all day Sunday. Many of them used marijuana regularly to relax after a long evening of study.

Dorm life was full of promiscuity and predatory sex. At registration I noticed how the upper class men hung around the incoming freshmen women like jackals surveying their prey. The women were away from home for the first time, a bit confused and anxious, flattered by the attention of seniors. Easy scores. As soon as classes began, the students petitioned me to eliminate dorm curfews and allow open co-ed dorms.

An epidemic of vandalism was turning the campus into a heap of rubble. The financial officer greeted me with a memo saying that if we could not reduce the rate of damage to college property, soon we would have to sell the campus for scrap.

Alcohol, drugs, sex, and destructive anger were symptomatic of pervasive loneliness and isolation in student life. Scores of students told me they had no friends on campus, no one at all to lean on when things got rough, no one to even talk to. Some didn't even know the names of other kids who lived on their hall in the dorms. Many were using alcohol and drugs to medicate their depression. Many of the one-night stands and promiscuous relationships were desperate and doomed attempts to find some kind of love and human concern.

The year before I came, ten students tried to kill themselves on the Steubenville campus. None succeeded, but I knew that some student eventually would commit suicide in that atmosphere of lonely desperation.

Bad as it was, student life at Steubenville was no worse than at other schools. Other college presidents told me that Steubenville's record of attempted suicide was not unusual. In fact, most presidents reported successful suicide attempts among their students and even more serious problems with alcohol, drugs, and promiscuous sex than we had.

The spiritual life of the campus was virtually non-existent. The dean of students and his associates sent a second petition to me shortly after the open-dorm request arrived. This one asked that the college cancel Sunday morning Mass in the chapel and retain only afternoon liturgies for the students who wanted to go. Attendance at morning Mass was poor, they said, because few were active Catholics and many stayed in bed Sunday morning to sleep off Saturday night's excesses.

As I mingled with students that fall, it became obvious to me that renewal at the college had to begin with changing their sad and lonely lives.

I made my first move on a Friday in December toward the end of the first semester.

I had worked out a plan in discussions with a president's council made up of major administrators, elected faculty, and students. However, the timing of announcing the changes was mine. I decided to hold a sudden meeting with little advance warning because many of the students were hostile toward authority. I didn't want them to have enough time to organize a boycott.

On a Friday I called the college's administrators into my office and told them I was calling a meeting of the entire college community for five o'clock that afternoon. I wanted everybody to be there and I wanted them to have time to think about what I would say. This was the Friday before first semester exams. The students would have three full weeks of Christmas vacation afterward to think about my plan.

Students and administrators were packed into the cafeteria when the meeting began. They lined the walls, sat in the aisles between tables, clustered at the doors. Seemingly, the only person left on campus who didn't attend the meeting was the woman who ran the college switchboard.

I began by referring to an earlier decision I had made about the proposal for cancelling Sunday morning Mass.

"I'm turning this down," I said. "Instead, I am taking over the Sunday liturgy myself. Mass is going to be about one and a half hours long. We're going to need the extra time for singing, praise, intercession, and preaching."

The assembly greeted this little announcement with silence.

Then I took up the student petition for open co-ed dorms and an end to curfews.

"This has some logic to it," I said. "Colleges across the country are moving this way. It's live-and-let-live. We have a lot of problems with the way we're living together now.

"But we're going to turn this around. I'm turning this petition down. Instead I want to do something very different to make life in the dorms a better place for everyone."

I talked about what I had seen in my months of getting to know students: the pervasive loneliness and isolation, the longing for friends and companionship, the need for support and encouragement, the cynicism, the desperation, the need for real fun instead of weekends spent in an alcoholic or drug haze.

Change had to begin with the way students actually lived, I said. It had to affect their relationships. I had an approach that I knew would work.

"Starting next fall, the dorms are going to be organized into households. Every student will belong to a small group. This group will have a leader. The students in the group will meet regularly for sharing, personal support, discussion of values and goals, and, I hope, prayer. We'll experiment with these households in the spring. By fall everyone will be in them. There will be no exceptions."

I talked only a little longer. I could see that students were incredulous. Some were angry. I took questions. The gist of most of them was that I had to be kidding. The gist of my answers was that no, I wasn't kidding at all. If you didn't want to be in a household, you had to find another place to go to school.

The plan went through on schedule. In the spring we developed basic household models for men and women and implemented them for everyone the next fall. The results were uneven. Where students participated reluctantly, the quality of sharing and prayer left much to be desired. Some households succeeded superbly well. Most students discovered that households worked better than they thought they would. My evaluation is that they did a great deal to break through the isolation of campus life. The household was a place where you could come and talk to some friends about whatever was on your mind. As the year wore on, more and more students discovered how nice this was.

Households were compulsory at Steubenville for three years. They are still an important part of campus life. Today the vast majority of our students choose to belong to one and almost all new students are part of a household for their first year or two.

Households were only part of the picture. In a sense, they

were a stopgap measure, a way to influence student life while buying time until other changes were in place. Student households did not constitute an environment of faith. It might support an environment of faith. It was part of an environment of faith. But a weekly meeting of students was hardly a fundamental change in the system.

A Scripture passage I often thought about when I prayed about faith was Matthew 21:21: "if you have faith and never doubt . . . even if you say to this mountain 'Be taken up and cast into the sea,' it will be done." This passage seems to point to one aspect of faith—that faith involves risk. Faith means stepping out and relying on the Lord Jesus Christ.

I decided to bring some people who had this kind of faith to Steubenville.

Over the years I got to know many people—priests, sisters, and laypeople—who seemed to have a desire to serve the Lord in radical faith. To them I made a radical invitation: Come to Steubenville and live together. I had a dorm that was empty because of declining enrollment. The previous administration was actually trying to sell it to private developers for office space. I told my friends I would take it off the market and let them live there if they would come and start a renewal center. The catch: I couldn't pay them anything directly. They would have to support themselves.

Five people responded to this mountain-into-the-sea invitation of faith at the beginning of the first year. One of them was Fr. Dave Tickerhoof, T.O.R., an old friend who oversaw the renewal center and has been at the college ever since. The next year Ann Shields joined them. Fr. Angelus Migliore, T.O.R., a classmate of mine, came that first year from the missions in Brazil and has been with me ever since. An average of twelve people lived at the center during the first two years.

These were exceptionally gifted people. They supported themselves by putting on renewal programs of all kinds—workshops, seminars, weekends, teaching conferences. They held programs at the college. Their teaching teams traveled as well, first regionally through the Ohio Valley and Pittsburgh area, then the East Coast, then nationally. Success fed on success. Within four years, twenty-five people were associated with the center.

These people of faith had an incalculable effect on the college. Students and faculty who were responding to the renewal of the college gravitated toward the renewal center; it was the rallying place for everyone who wanted to make or renew a serious commitment to the Lord. At first the life of the center was a counterculture in the midst of the worldly secular culture of the campus. As the years passed, it grew in strength and confidence. At some point in the late 1970s, the charismatic, faith-filled life of the center became the dominant culture on campus.

The renewal center's programs made the College of Steubenville an international Catholic conference center. The first conference was held in 1976 when the National Service Committee of the Catholic Charismatic Renewal asked us to hold a conference for priests. Three weeks before the conference, Fr. Philip Bebie, the conference administrator, came into my office with a problem: so many priests had already registered that the largest auditorium on campus could not hold the conference. I recalled an amazing experience I had had the summer before in Bergen, New York, when I preached in a tent with a team of Pentecostal ministers.

"Rent a big tent," I said.

The tent has gone up in June every summer since then. We have had conferences for priests and nuns, businessmen and young people, people interested in prophecy and healing, and prayer group leaders. The conferences have brought the college to the attention of renewal-minded adults and young people from all over the world.

The young people's conference in particular profoundly influenced the college. Every summer thousands of young

Catholics descend on the campus for a weekend of Spirit-filled ministry. Invariably, this weekend is marked by healings, miracles, deliverance, conversions, filling with the Holy Spirit, and inspirational teachings. Inevitably, many students seeking a lively spiritual environment enroll in school, further building and reinforcing the environment of faith.

Indeed, the college's approach to student recruitment was one of the first policies to be radically overhauled when I arrived. When competition for students intensified in the late 1960s and early 1970s, Steubenville responded in the conventional ways. Recruiters talked with high school guidance counselors, visited high school college nights, worked on establishing special relationships with Catholic high schools in western Ohio and eastern Pennsylvania, and advertised in the Catholic press.

We virtually abandoned all these techniques. Our people went out first as proclaimers of the good news, secondly as recruiters for the College of Steubenville. They traveled nationally, speaking at charismatic prayer meetings and days of renewal instead of college nights, staying in friends' homes instead of hotels, talking about the college as a place where the Spirit-filled life is lived radically instead of as a place where young people can have fun while preparing for a well-paying job.

This approach eventually brought more students and a different kind of student to the campus—but not immediately.

The freshman class entering the first year after I took over as president was the smallest in the college's history. Morale fell to record lows among many members of the college community. One professor, noting the decline in admissions, proposed to a key committee that we start getting the students ready to enroll in new colleges in view of the inevitable closure of the College of Steubenville. Two other young faculty members called a private meeting of the faculty and proposed a motion of no confidence in my leadership.

These protests did not get anywhere, but the main reason was the lack of any viable alternative rather than overwhelming confidence in my policies. Renewal was purchased painfully, at a high price.

Most of the pain was human.

The five top administrators left by their decision or mine during my first two years as president. In the following five years the people I hand-picked to succeed them also left. Some left because they couldn't do the job that needed to be done, some because they couldn't in conscience support the new direction for the school, some because they couldn't take the heat from faculty, students, and alumni who opposed the new direction.

A few **felt be**trayed. I remember with anguish a priest who left the college because I was imposing a vision of Franciscan life that differed greatly from his. His vision was not wrong, just different, too different for peaceful coexistence or compromise.

I made mistakes in my judgments about people. Some of my changes did not work well. Very often, other people paid a greater price for my mistakes than I did.

The turnover in administrators added to the confusion. Decisions and reforms in many areas were delayed for months and even years until the right person with the right vision was in place. My deliberate decision to deal with the academic side of the college after attending to the spiritual atmosphere and student life inevitably meant that necessary changes were postponed. The board of trustee's decision to abandon a successful but costly men's basketball program caused great resentment among some alumni and friends in the region. The outcry about basketball was so great that I decided to concentrate my fund-raising efforts on the new friends of the college who put a higher value on spiritual renewal.

Renewal is seldom a matter of abandoning the dead for the living, but rather of forsaking the good for the better.

Everyone supports renewal in the abstract. When the details come along, people differ. And whatever path to renewal is chosen, some people will pay a high price for change. Often the institution will pay a price too.

These are among the lessons of the first years of rebuilding the Lord's house at the College of Steubenville.

FIFTEEN

The Way, the Truth, and the Life

O NE DAY, AFTER I HAD BEEN PRESIDENT of the University of Steubenville for about a decade, I was thinking about the problem of explaining renewal. Renewal is hard to define, hard to talk about, hard to describe.

I picked up the Bible and leafed through it.

The source of the wisdom we need lies in the word of God—the word of Scripture which reveals the Word incarnate. The depth of Scripture's wisdom is endless. The most familiar passages reveal ever-deeper and ever-richer meanings if we merely pay attention to the leading of the Holy Spirit every time we read them.

My eyes fell on a very familiar passage: Jesus said "I am the way, the truth, and the life." How often had I read these words silently to myself in the course of daily Scripture reading. How often had I read them aloud from the pulpit at Mass. They have a nice rhythm: way, truth, life. They mean, of course, that the Lord Jesus is truly Lord. He possesses all; he provides all; he is the way to the Father.

But way, truth, and life are meaningful concepts, not merely symbolic terms meaning everything. Every group of Christians who are seeking to follow the Lord needs the way, the truth, and the life. Renewal in large part consists of restoring the Lord's plan to each of these dimensions of life.

We can use these words to talk about the changes at the University of Steubenville.

The *life* is the power of the Holy Spirit—the essential breath of God that ignites the fire of his love in our hearts. Without the Spirit we have nothing except our desires and ideas, which is to say nothing except the corrupt nature from which we need redemption.

The *way* is the structure of life, the pattern of living that is shaped around God's plan for human life. Without the structure of the way, the fire of the Spirit will shoot off wildly without direction and eventually peter out—something that often happens in the charismatic renewal.

The *truth* is correct knowledge of what God has revealed about his relationship with man. We must understand the world God made, the predicament man finds himself in, and the provision God made to deliver us from it.

We are in trouble if we lack any of these three, yet we also face difficulties if any one of them is overstressed.

Truth without life and cast loose from the way becomes empty speculation, a mental exercise, and a word game. Many Catholic colleges and universities are plagued by this sterile pursuit of mental abstractions.

A way of living divorced from truth and emptied of the life of the Spirit becomes legalism. By themselves, commitments and courses and systems become a set of rules, as dry and as nourishing as dust. We often see this in the church and in renewal movements: people going through the motions, wondering why they are continuing to go to meetings.

The enthusiasm of the life of the Spirit will eventually fade without the purpose and direction of the way and the truth. Indeed, the fire of the Spirit has often gone out in renewal movements.

We need all three—the way, the truth, *and* the life. The trick is to keep everything in balance. This isn't easy. Fortunately, we have a model—the Lord Jesus Christ who *is* at once the way, the truth, and the life. No system, no formula, no framework, no management program or problem-solving technique will successfully bring us to the place where the Lord wants us to be. Only he can do that.

We recognized the need for balance among the changes at the college as soon as I started households as an early step in building an environment of faith. Dozens of students complained. They told me they couldn't possibly share their lives with others in the way I described. Some were paralyzed with fear by the idea of having to tell other young people about their struggles and values and hopes.

These were legitimate complaints. Many students simply didn't know the first thing about how to talk openly and personally to people in a group. Neither did they know how Christians handle their emotions, organize their time, settle differences, get to know members of the opposite sex, or simply how to have a good time on a night off.

Most students are as ignorant about these basic lessons of practical Christian living as they were about nursing or engineering or French literature or the other academic subjects that they came to college to learn when they enrolled as freshmen. They need to be *taught* these things, just as they need to be taught the academic subjects that will lead to a degree. A Christian college has the responsibility of teaching young people not just to learn how to make a living but also to learn how to live. Christianity is a way of life. It is no accident that the early Christians were called followers of "the way."

We made a large investment in efforts to teach "the way" as soon as the first major changes in the college were completed. Over the years, we expanded the campus ministry staff from one half-time person to five full-time people plus additional part-time staff and interns, and then we integrated them with student life. These men and women provide instruction in the basics of the Christian life, as well as in practical details of Christian living. Students learn about prayer, Scripture study, overcoming personal problems. They also learn about dating, growing in Christian character, relating to other single people, and other practical topics.

The campus ministers also pay attention to "the life"—the fire of the Holy Spirit. About ninety percent of our resident students are baptized in the Spirit by the end of any given school year. That's an astonishing statistic, one that humbles me before the faithfulness of God. Young men and women at the college are attracted to this experience by the witness of the lives of the people they see around them. Peer pressure works in the opposite direction than in most schools—toward the Lord rather than away from him, toward a stronger, not weaker, Christian commitment, toward maturity in Christ and away from the foolishness of the world.

Most of the people who work in campus ministry and student life are members of the Servants of Christ the King, a group of three hundred Christians in the Steubenville area who have made a covenant commitment to live their Christian lives together and to take responsibility for each other. The community consists of both married and single lay people, plus some nuns and priests like myself. The members of the community meet weekly in men's and women's groups for mutual support, sharing, and prayer, just as the majority of Steubenville students do in their dorm households. We also worship together every week and support a number of local and regional outreaches. I meet weekly with Tom Kneier and Keith Fournier, university alumni who oversee the community along with myself and other, newer coordinators.

The community contributes invaluable service to the university. Members of the community moderate every household on campus; their responsibilities include giving direction, teaching, counseling, and acting as general overseers. The community also provides the recruitment pool for entrance level administrators, provides the staff for the conference office, and is a great asset in recruiting faculty who want to be associated with a Christian community.

One of the first people I sat down with after coming to Steubenville was the academic dean. Several men had held the job since I had, and I had lost touch with the faculty, departments, and curriculum. He told me what was happening on the academic side of the college.

Fewer students were majoring in the humanities, more in business, engineering, and other vocationally-oriented specialties. The number of history and English majors was way down; some faculty in those departments were worried about their jobs.

Business and education were popular. The dean thought computers were the coming thing, a prediction that was right on the mark, and he thought the college would have to offer an attractive specialty in data processing if it was to be competitive in the future.

"How about philosophy?" I asked.

"Very little interest. It is no longer required. One student majored in philosophy last year, a double philosophy and math major. A great student. He wants to go into computers."

"And theology?"

The dean smiled a bitter smile. He was a priest, a Franciscan educated like I had been. He loved the great theologians.

"Theology is minimal here, Mike," he said. "We still require two courses, but even that's resented. We don't even have a full-time professor in the so-called theology department. It's actually part of the philosophy department. We don't offer a theology major. Some faculty even want to reduce the theology requirement."

I knew theology was in a bad way in Catholic colleges, but I was genuinely surprised that Steubenville had no major and was even considering reducing the theology requirement. I recalled my interview with the search committee, and my ringing promise to put spiritual matters above anything else—especially academic and financial concerns. Here was a chance to honor that promise: we needed a theology major and a vibrant department.

The key to restoring theology to its rightful place of prominence in the curriculum was getting the right people to come and teach it. One man in particular was invaluable: Fr. Daniel Sinisi. Fr. Dan was professor of moral theology at St. Francis Seminary and a covenant brother of mine during my years as rector. Fr. Dan agreed to come to Steubenville and become chairman of a rejuvenated theology department.

Other key faculty who joined the department in the early years were Fr. Francis Martin and Fr. Roland Faley. Dr. Alan Schreck and Fr. John Bertolucci added great richness in the area of pastoral theology. I met Fr. Francis in Rome in 1975. I never met anyone who spoke about the word of God with such power. I was delighted when he agreed to join the faculty as well. Alan Schreck had been a brilliant student and renewal leader at Notre Dame before studying for his doctorate at St. Michael's in Toronto.

The restoration of theology's academic eminence has been remarkable. By the mid-1980s, theology had become the most popular major in the university. I don't have the figures to prove it, but I suspect that the University of Steubenville is the only university in the country where theology is the most popular major. I do know that in 1985, there were twice as many theology majors at Steubenville than at Catholic University or Notre Dame.

Theology became preeminent for several reasons. We began to attract the kind of student who was seriously interested in studying the intellectual underpinnings of his or her faith. We also offered dual-major programs whereby students could major in both theology and a career-oriented specialty in four years. But theology also grew because in a dozen subtle ways the university became a place where the study of the things of God was honored. The intellectual life of the campus was deeply affected by a theological perspective. Theologians exerted influence in academic affairs. Theology at the university has become what John Henry Newman called it—the Queen of the Sciences.

Other academic developments have been gratifying. In 1980 the college became a university when it began offering graduate degrees in business and theology. By the beginning of 1985 two computer science majors were operating. In 1984 our Christian nursing program was fully chartered by the state of Ohio and in 1985 it received the highest accreditation possible from the National League of Nursing.

The nursing program is a good example of our strenuous effort to build a Christian vision into academic work wherever possible. The program meets the highest secular academic standards; all the students who have graduated from it have been employed immediately. But a Christian perspective is built into the very fabric of the program. Every nursing student takes a course in spiritual healing and studies death and dying from a Christian point of view.

The same thing is true of business administration. We teach a Christian perspective on business while offering a professionally impressive degree. For example, the teaching includes a perspective on labor relations, on reconciliation of differences, on capital and social responsibility.

In a broad sense, we are striving to integrate all that we do at Steubenville into a unifying vision. Human life is splitting apart today. Church is separated from state. Communities of people who once shared a common life divide, divide, and divide again. Sacred knowledge and secular learning have nothing to do with each other. Even secular knowledge has shattered into specialties, subspecialities, and sub-subspecialties, with specialists unable to explain to outsiders what they are doing or why they are doing it.

Most universities today reflect the chaotic fragmentation of society. We are striving to make Steubenville a place where all the diverse intellectual and social activities that go on in an institution of higher education find a unifying direction and purpose. In the broadest sense, this vision is the word of God—the revelation of God and of God's plan for human life. In a narrower sense, our purpose is to train students for a difficult contest with forces that seek to undermine faith, the moral life, and God's word.

Word of what the Lord has done at the university has gotten around. Hundreds of visitors have come to the campus looking for help with their problems. Many are professional youth ministers looking for some way to "get through to the kids." They are impressed by the obvious spiritual vitality of the campus. Some are administrators of Christian colleges and universities who are grappling with fearsome cultural and financial pressures. They wonder how we can do the exact opposite of what most schools have done and still show growth in numbers and support. Some want to renew parishes, seminaries, prayer groups, high schools. They want to know our secret.

To all of them I give some version of the story I have just told. Build an environment of faith. Take care of your primary constituency. Get good people to join you. Expect opposition. Seek the Lord. When you hear him speak, do whatever is necessary to obey him.

I also tell them that they have to be willing to pay the price of renewal. Renewal movements run out of steam and church institutions become less and less successful at doing what they are supposed to for one simple reason: those who have responsibility for them are unwilling to pay the price of significant renewal. Those responsible often know what needs to be done. They are usually good people who sincerely want to do the Lord's will. But for any number of reasons, some of them quite plausible and even persuasive, they don't make the unpopular decisions and commit the resources necessary to achieve their goals.

Numerous people made innumerable difficult decisions over the years to make student life, the academic program, and spiritual life on campus more pleasing to God. Many of these were risky decisions: decisions to spend money we didn't have to hire campus ministers and key faculty, decisions to risk alienating many students and their parents by fostering a charismatic spirituality, decisions to make theology our academic priority, decisions my friends made when they came without pay to set up a renewal center, decisions to radically alter the character of an institution that had a loyal constituency, decisions to make changes that ran contrary to the whole direction of academic and religious life in twentieth century America, decisions that caused one's friends and peers at other universities to laugh when they heard what was going on at Steubenville.

Renewal comes only when it's made the highest priority. It has to come before financial concerns, before loyalty to one's staff and supporters, even before survival itself. Most people who run institutions aren't willing to do this. When it gets right down to a tough choice, most presidents, pastors, and chief executives will put something ahead of renewal.

Nearly all the people who come to Steubenville asking about renewal are the campus ministers or the student life director—almost never the president or top administrators who make the priority decisions about money, staff, and resources. That's significant, and sad. This is a time of enormous blessings. God is pouring out his Holy Spirit in abundance. This is the time to renew. This is the time to be bound together with others who put the highest priority on Jesus Christ and his lordship over us.

Back in 1974, God called me to a particular job when I heard him ask, "What if I want you to become president of the College of Steubenville?" That was tremendously freeing. I have done many jobs in my life. Never before had I had the conviction that my work was "of God" to the degree that I do now. When I was dean I plunged into the task of solving a thousand problems—and exhausted myself (and others). I approached the job of being rector of the seminary more sensibly, but even then I did not particularly know that the charge to do the job was from God.

I think the Lord has a particular job for every one of us. He has a lot of work to do, and we are the only ones he has to do it. He needs evangelists, pastors, teachers, and missionaries; he needs strong families, homes that are open to guests, and business people who can make money for the Kingdom.

People sometimes ask me what I do as president. Fr. Jim Ferry once called my role "the keeper of the vision." God supplies the vision and I proclaim it; initiate its implementation in constantly new areas; reinforce it; correct, admonish, pastor, and encourage based on it; and sell it to benefactors, faculty candidates and potential students. I also pray a lot and I try to hear what the Lord wants next for the university.

All of this is like tending a garden. The flowers are planted there, bursting with potential but also facing dangers that would snuff them out. My job is to protect and nurture them while the Lord does his work. When the students are tended properly, they blossom. For my part, I watch in awe, praising God.

SIXTEEN

The Body of My Son Is Broken

THE LORD'S COMMAND TO "REBUILD MY CHURCH" is an ecumenical command that requires a commitment to Christian unity. The Catholic church is not the only church that needs rebuilding. In fact, renewal of the Catholic church will not be complete unless it encompasses a vision of the unity of the body of Christ.

I came to this vision through my involvement in the Catholic charismatic renewal. Kevin Ranaghan and Ralph Martin, who later served as trustees of the university, and other early Catholic charismatic leaders had powerful ecumenical experiences at the very beginning of the movement. Protestants prayed with many of them to be baptized in the Spirit, taught them about spiritual gifts, advised them about growing in the Spirit, and enriched their theological understanding of this outpouring of grace and power.

I had no such ecumenical experience. My education was either wholly Catholic or wholly secular. The Protestants I knew in college and law school were almost all non-practicing Christians. I received a pre-Vatican II Catholic education in grammar school and an entirely Catholic formation in the seminary. I do not remember reading Protestant theologians or hearing any lectures by Protestant academics. I came to ordination with many of the prejudices and stereotypes about Protestants that Catholics of my generation typically had.

The stereotypes began to break down as I worked and prayed with Protestant ministers and lay people while dean of the College of Steubenville. Getting to know Protestants personally made the difference. I discovered that the beliefs we hold in common are more extensive and more important than the beliefs that divide us. I also had to admit that Protestants did some things better than Catholics did. They read and studied the Bible more, usually had greater commitments to their church congregations, and often had a closer personal relationship with the Lord.

My last defenses crumbled in 1973 during an ecumenical retreat for Catholic and Protestant leaders in the charismatic renewal. Appropriately, the weapon that destroyed them was repentance.

We wanted to end the retreat with a common liturgy, a desire that brought us face to face with the reality of the division of the body of Christ. Even though we had come to love each other as individuals, we could not fully participate in each other's worship services. We decided to have a foot washing service. Anyone who wanted to express repentance for prejudice against another denomination could come forward and wash the feet of his brothers as a sign of sorrow.

I wept as men whom I loved as brothers came forward to wash my feet. They repented for teaching that Catholics were not Christians, that the pope was the anti-Christ and the church was the whore of Babylon, that Catholic piety was crude superstition.

I, in turn, washed the feet of my Pentecostal, Lutheran, and Presbyterian brothers. I asked their forgiveness for teaching that hardly anyone outside the Catholic church could be saved, for making jokes about Martin Luther and other great reformers, for my smug disdain for the piety of Pentecostal worship. They wept as I repented.

The service went on for about four hours. Then Derek Prince, a Pentecostal teacher of imposing demeanor, began singing the Battle Hymn of the Republic. We all joined in, then marched around the room singing lustily. We had repented to each other, forgiven each other, and were now experiencing the joy of repentance. We were carried away by a vision of the power and beauty of the unified body of Christ. Unity did not fully exist, but I tasted what unity would be like when it did. Since then, the vision of Christian unity has been an integral part of my work.

To catch this vision is to feel pain because of the current divided state of the church. I never felt this pain more intensely than I did in 1977 at an interdenominational charismatic conference in Kansas City. This unprecedented event was an occasion for rejoicing. The planning committee represented fourteen denominations, and more than 50,000 Christians, about half of them Catholics, gathered for fellowship, teaching, and prayer. Nevertheless, sorrow made the most vivid impression, because the conference displayed the division of the church for all to see.

The Father himself spoke of this pain in a prophecy at the last general session in Arrowhead Stadium. I will never forget it. This is what he said:

Mourn and weep for the body of my Son is broken. Mourn and weep for the body of my Son is broken. Come before me with sackcloth and ashes. Come before me with tears and mourning for the body of my Son is broken. I would have made you one new man but the body of my Son is broken. I would have made you a light on a mountaintop, a city glorious and splendorous that all the world would have seen, but the body of my Son is broken.

The light is dim. My people are scattered. The body of my Son is broken. I gave all that I had in the body and blood of my Son. It spilled on the earth. The body of my Son is broken. Turn from the sins of your fathers and walk in the ways of my Son. Return to the plan of your Father. Return to the purpose of your God. The body of my Son is broken. Mourn and weep, for the body of my Son is broken.

We obeyed; we mourned and wept. We wept for our distrust of one another, for our cruel jokes, for our ignorance and bigotry, for our indifference and dislike and outright hostility. We begged God to forgive us, and then we prayed for an outpouring of his Spirit that would make us one. I was the next speaker after this prophecy. I knew I had heard God. I discarded my text and talked about obeying what we had just heard.

It is literally true that the body of the Son is broken. The church *is* the body of Christ and the church lies shattered and bleeding in thousands of pieces. As we come to know the Lord more personally, we will inevitably experience and grieve over his broken body. As he leads us into renewal and service, we will inevitably find ourselves working to repair the divisions of Christianity.

That is why movements of authentic renewal have an ecumenical dimension. In recent years the Cursillo, Marriage Encounter, and the charismatic renewal have developed an ecumenical dimension after first blossoming as Catholic renewal movements. Movements to renew Catholic worship, social outreach, music, and Scripture study have drawn strength and inspiration from Protestant sources.

So has the renewal of the University of Steubenville. From the beginning, a commitment to Christian unity and a thoroughly ecumenical vision has been an integral part of the Lord's work on the campus.

We express this commitment in many ways. No theology major can graduate without studying John Wesley and Methodism, renewal movements outside the Catholic church, and the contribution the reformers made to theology and worship. Catholic theology by definition encompasses every authentic leading of God's Spirit, including those that occur outside the Catholic church.

A significant number of Steubenville students are not Catholics. Many of them are sons and daughters of Episcopalian priests and ministers who have attended our annual priests' conference—another event with an ecumenical character.

For many years, evangelical Protestants associated with the Christian Coalition have worked with our students as dorm directors. These young graduates, mostly from covenant Presbyterian colleges, worked closely with our campus ministers in teaching our students the basics of practical Christian living and in leading them to a deeper spiritual life.

One of the most popular features of college life was a program that brought Protestant charismatic preachers to campus for a regular "preaching night." The anointing of the Holy Spirit often fell on these thoroughly interdenominational services held in the campus chapel.

The Servants of Christ the King sponsors the Ohio Valley Christian Association, an evangelistic ecumenical outreach that seeks to lead people in the region to an initial or renewed commitment to the Lord.

In 1984, the Servants of Christ the King became part of a larger international ecumenical community called the Sword of the Spirit. We did this in response to a strong sense that God was calling us to make a formal commitment to a body that was itself ecumenical in composition and is committed to working for Christian unity.

Our lives would be much simpler if we did not have to do this ecumenical work.

Unexpected problems keep coming up. We have to work hard to communicate with each other. There are cultural barriers to overcome, embarrassing moments to endure. Misunderstandings abound. Progress seems slow. Christian unity seems far off.

If we did not do ecumenical work, I wouldn't have to correct Catholic friends who want unity right now and others who think our differences are so great that ecumenical activity is wasted. We could easily spend all our time on purely Catholic matters. The Lord knows there is plenty of work to do in our Catholic world where the people and the problems are familiar.

We do it because we reach a point in our relationship with the Lord where we cannot avoid it. We grieve over his broken body, but we also realize that our unity is real. "There is one body and one Spirit," Paul writes to the Ephesians, "one Lord, one faith, one baptism, one God and Father of us all."

This is not simply an abstract "theological" truth. Many substantial and enduring issues divide Christians, but the beliefs we share in common are more numerous and more important. All men and women who have been baptized in the name of the Father, Son, and Spirit, who affirm that they pray by the one Spirit, and who believe that the Bible is the inspired word of God are our brothers and sisters.

This unity already exists. It cries out for practical expression.

Once at a conference of Christian pastors I heard a minister give an inspiring and, to me, somewhat amazing appeal. He had just received an urgent message from a Jewish Christian friend in Israel, he said. This man had some disturbing information about the plight of Christians in Lebanon: Arab Christians were being killed by Muslim terrorists and gunmen in ever-increasing numbers. Danger to the Christians was increasing. This Jewish Christian was appealing to Christians around the world to give aid to their Lebanese brothers and sisters, to pray for their safety, and to use what influence they might have to induce Western governments to give them protection.

Here was Christian unity in action—a Jew pleading for the protection of Arabs. Their nations were at war; their peoples had been locked in bitter struggle for centuries, but their one faith in Jesus Christ transcended the walls between them. This is the kind of solidarity all Christians should have.

In recent years, Christians have been experiencing this solidarity in some unexpected places. Back in the 1950s, Harry Blamires, the British lay theologian, made a controversial and darkly prophetic prediction. "In the near future," he wrote, "the dominating controversy within Christendom will be between those who give full weight to the supernatural reality at the heart of all Christian dogma, practice, and thought, and those who try to convert Christianity into a naturalistic religion by whittling away the reality and comprehensiveness of its supernatural basis."

Blamires's prediction has come to pass. We are in what my good friend Ralph Martin calls "a crisis of truth." Ever since the Reformation, Christianity has been divided by theological disputes over authority in the church, the nature of inspiration, and the proper way to formulate doctrines. Today, however, Christians are divided by fundamental questions of truth. Did Jesus really preach a message of salvation? Did his death on the cross atone for our sins and did he literally rise from the dead? Can we know *anything* for certain?

Sadly, many Christians answer no to these questions. For them the gospel of Jesus Christ is at best a part of the truth, an inspiration, perhaps, for personal fulfillment or political liberation.

As Harry Blamires predicted, ecumenical alliances are shifting as this struggle for the integrity and authority of the gospel continues in the church. I have found friends and allies in unexpected places, particularly among Protestant evangelicals. Frankly, my beliefs about the essentials of the gospel are closer to those of evangelical Protestants who are culturally very different from me than they are to the beliefs of some Catholics whom I grew up with and have known and worked with for years. I regret this, but I am not surprised by it. We are united by one life in Jesus Christ, not by a shared human culture. The word of God transcends cultures and nations and tongues. It takes priority over human preferences and smashes man-made barriers.

I am reminded of this every time a Protestant or Orthodox brother or sister gives me some personal support or enriches my understanding of the gospel I preach and the Lord I serve.

This has happened often, more and more often as the years go by.

This shouldn't surprise us either, because no one church or denomination or theological tradition contains all of God's truth. We need each other in order to possess the fullness of God's truth.

The Protestant Reformation was a catalyst for a Catholic restoration movement which corrected real deficiencies in the Catholic church. Many Catholic preachers and teachers had distorted teaching on indulgences, failed to preach God's word with power, and failed to emphasize the fact that we are justified by faith in the Lord Jesus. In some places, Catholic worship had become mixed with superstitious practices and mechanical prayer. The Protestant reformers highlighted these conditions, but the changes they initiated have still not been completely assimilated.

The average churchgoing Protestant, for example, knows more about the Bible than the average serious Catholic. It's also fair to say that most Protestants hear a better sermon in church on Sunday than most Catholics do.

At the same time, the Catholic church has preserved a richness in worship, truths about the role of Mary and the saints, and a principle of unity and universality that other traditions lack.

Back in the early 1960s I was excited when the fathers of Vatican II declined to identify the church of Jesus Christ with the Catholic church. The Council taught that the church of Jesus Christ "subsists" in the Catholic church. This means that the church of Jesus Christ embraces the Catholic church as well as all authentic reforms. I understood this theologically at the time. Now I understand it practically, as a day-to-day truth. To accomplish everything God wants of us, we need each other—Catholic, Protestant, and Orthodox alike supporting each other, enriching each other, and working together to do the Lord's work.

Building Christian unity means that we must roll up our sleeves and get down to work with Christians from other churches. We must get to know other Christians personally.

This is hard to do. We will always be able to find a hundred reasons why we can't do it. Time is short. Other demands press on our time.

There's another reason. Satan does not want Christians to work effectively together. The scandal of the division of Christianity is a great asset for the kingdom of darkness. The power that a united church would possess is a great threat to him. Therefore, Satan will do anything to prevent meaningful cooperation among us.

For all these reasons, Christians must fortify their resolve to make Christian unity amount to something more than an occasional ecumenical prayer service for peace. Cardinal Mercier, the great Belgian ecumenist who led the way in ecumenical cooperation earlier in this century, had a handy formula for unity. "We have to encounter one another in order to know one another," he said. "We have to know one another in order to love one another. We have to love one another in order to unite."

Unity is in the future. I have the barest glimmer of an idea of how it will take place. Today, however, we can encounter each other and love each other. It's essential that we do this. "Complete my joy," writes Paul, "by being of the same mind, having the same love, being in full accord and of one mind."

SEVENTEEN

God's Family

THE WORLD IS FULL OF UNHAPPY FAMILIES. I know. Almost every day I counsel people who grew up in deficient families years ago, who are growing up in them now, or who head such families today. Many of them think that somewhere the ideal family exists, that they were unlucky in drawing the family they did. I tell them they're wrong, that no family works the way it should.

But I can understand the pain they feel. You see, I am a product of an unhappy family too, and I have seen how God can heal the deepest wounds and make up for the greatest deficiencies in our upbringing.

My father left my mother when I was three years old. He then left the country to run an export-import business in Mexico City. He paid for my college and law school, but he was never a father to me.

Bill, my mother's second husband, preferred not to have me around too much. I was sent to boarding schools. When he found out that I didn't want my mother to marry him, he turned on me in a rage. He hated the fact that I was a devout Catholic and he mocked and reviled the church every time I came home for a visit.

My mother was a woman caught in the middle, between her husband and her son, between her Catholic beliefs and the second marriage that excluded her from the sacraments. A great sadness blighted her life.

It wasn't much of a family.

When I was a student I often dreaded the weekends. Should I go home for a visit, sleep in the living room, and argue with Bill or should I stay at school and be lonely? I grew strong through this adversity, but I didn't choose it and would have gladly given it up. I buried resentment deep inside. Why couldn't I have a normal happy family like everyone else?

The day before I entered the Franciscans I told Bill and my mother about my plans. She wept; he disgustedly told me that I was wasting my life. I entered the Franciscans with a strong sense of having burned my bridges behind me.

In the seminary, however, I began to turn my family over to the Lord. Power broke into my prayer the day I heard the Lord tell me that he loved my mother more than I did. I prayed for my mother constantly, more than once a day. I asked the Lord to have mercy on her and Bill and on my father. I interceded for them. I asked the Lord to bring all three of them to himself.

And miracle of miracles—he did.

My mother and Bill entered a celibate brother-sister relationship and she returned to the sacraments. She spent most of the last year of her life in contemplative prayer. She had visions and mystical experiences that closely resembled those of the great mystical saints. Her death in 1961 was simply a matter of stripping away the thin veil that still separated her from God.

Then Bill Robertson became a Catholic. During a stay in the hospital the great enemy of the church met a priest he liked. They had many long discussions. It all started to make sense to Bill. He took instructions and was received into the Catholic church.

My father returned to the church as well several years before he died in 1968.

There was one more great family blessing, and it happened inside me.

Just before Holy Week, 1978, I was summoned to Bill's

hospital bed in Fort Lauderdale. He was dying. I was the only family he had. Decisions had to be made about his treatment, difficult decisions. Bill had to prepare for death. I was acutely aware of the responsibility I had. Whatever grace and blessing Bill received would most likely come through me. Every day during Holy Week I was conscious of my burdens as I drove from his apartment to the hospital in the morning and back again at night.

On Good Friday evening I was driving home through one of the entertainment districts of Fort Lauderdale when I suddenly found myself in the grip of a nearly uncontrollable urge to park the car and sample some of the pleasures that surrounded me. I was mesmerized by the bright neon lights, enchanted by the sights and sounds of decadence. It would be so easy to stop, so much fun if I did.

It was the most powerful temptation I ever experienced. Only the most brutal act of the will kept me driving the car straight down the road until I got home.

Trembling with fright, I closed the door of my room, sat down, and tried to understand what had happened to me. I was alone in a strange city, always a reason to be careful and take extra precautions. I was distracted and possibly emotionally drained by caring for a dying man whom I was close to. Caring for Bill had also stirred up memories of the past, not all of them pleasant ones. All this left my defenses down. I was blindsided by the Tempter, like a quarterback who is looking the other way when a blitzing linebacker hammers him to the turf.

But that wasn't all. The Lord spoke to me about a more fundamental problem.

"You are acting as if I am not with you," he said. "You are reaching, pleading, pushing to get to me. You are serving on your own power. You are trying to do things *for* me rather than *in* me.

"The truth is that I am with you. I am your family. I am in you. Start living in the family."

That moment was a breakthrough in my understanding of who God is and who I am in relation to him. God is family. The Son is always giving glory to the Father. The Father is always saying he is pleased with the Son. The Holy Spirit is the bond of love between them.

The three members of this family are always praying in me, just as they pray in you and in everyone who has been reborn in Jesus Christ. We are never alone. We never need to fear. We always have our family with us.

We don't reach out to God in prayer. Rather we enter into the prayer that is going on within us ceaselessly.

We don't look outside ourselves for healing. We receive the healing graces that flow from the Holy Trinity.

We don't struggle to bring God's love to our families, friends, and co-workers. Rather, we participate in what God is already doing to bring his grace to those around us.

Best of all, the Father is a Father to us just as he was Father to Jesus, for that is exactly what it means to be sons and daughters of God.

This truth penetrated my dim consciousness one summer evening during a talk at a priests' conference at the University of Steubenville. The speaker was Fr. Raniero Cantalamessa, a Capuchin Franciscan who is the preacher to the papal household, more commonly known as the pope's preacher. At one point Fr. Raniero got inspired, as you might think the pope's preacher often would. He was talking about who we are in relation to the Father, how we should pray, what we should expect. We should pray, he said, as sons going before the Father with the Son, saying: "Father, I am your Jesus."

"Father, I am your Jesus." It sounds peculiar, even faintly blasphemous. But we have exactly the relationship with the Father that allows us to speak these words. We stand before him precisely as Jesus did—and does. We are sons and daughters of the Father. We can approach him in the same way Jesus did. He will use us as he used Jesus.

The family of God makes up for everything lacking in our

natural families. When I finally accepted the Lord's outstretched hand and entered the family of God, I received everything missing from my home life and upbringing as a child. My father, mother, and Bill were with the Lord—and so was I. That relationship was all that mattered, and it contained everything that any of us need.

That relationship contains everything we need as we go forth to do the works of God in the world. We are servants of a Master who has a lot to do. There's a war going on. We are both the army and the battlefield. The stakes are the highest—eternal life for millions upon millions of human beings. Yet we can proceed with cheerful confidence because we are in God's family. The Father directs us, the Spirit empowers us, and the Son stands with us. We are God's sons and daughters, in whom he is well pleased. And his delight is to proclaim of us, as he did of Jesus, "This is my beloved Son in whom I am well pleased."

For information regarding the Franciscan University of Steubenville or any of its programs write:

Office of the President
The Franciscan University of Steubenville
Steubenville, Ohio 43952